A Kid's Guide to Fandom

A Kid's Guide to Fandom

EXPLORING FAN-FIC, COSPLAY, GAMING, PODCASTING, AND MORE IN THE GEEK WORLD!

Written by **AMY RATCLIFFE**

Illustrated by **DAVE PERILLO**

RP KIDS
PHILADELPHIA

Running Press Kids
Hachette Book Group
1290 Avenue of the Americas, New York, NY 10104
www.runningpress.com/rpkids
@RP_Kids

Printed in China

First Edition: May 2021

Published by Running Press Kids, an imprint of Perseus Books, LLC,
a subsidiary of Hachette Book Group, Inc. The Running Press Kids name
and logo is a trademark of the Hachette Book Group.

The Hachette Speakers Bureau provides a wide range of authors for
speaking events. To find out more, go to www.hachettespeakersbureau.com
or call (866) 376-6591.

The publisher is not responsible for websites (or their content)
that are not owned by the publisher.

Print book cover and interior design by Marissa Raybuck.

Library of Congress Control Number: 2020946885

ISBNs: 978-0-7624-9875-8 (paperback), 978-0-7624-9877-2 (ebook)

1010

10 9 8 7 6 5 4 3 2 1

For all who squee

Contents

Introduction: What Is Fandom?.. 01

What Kind of Fan Are You? Quiz 05

09
Chapter 1
Pen and Paper

31
Chapter 2
Playing the Part

47
Chapter 3
Hey, Listen

67
Chapter 4
Press Start

83
Chapter 5
So Say We All

99
Chapter 6
Going on an Adventure

Conclusion: The End of This Story (and the Beginning of Your Journey
 in Fandom) 117

This Is My Fandom! Sheet 119

Fan Character Sheet 121

Fandom Glossary 125

Extra Materials and Resources 129

Acknowledgments 133

About the Author & Illustrator 134

A Kid's Guide
to Fandom

What Is Fandom?

CLOSE YOUR EYES. WAIT—NOT YET.

First, think about all the books you read, the games you play, the movies and TV shows you watch. Okay, now close your eyes and go through those stories in your mind. What characters pop into your head? Are you picturing a scene or moment that you adore? What are some of your favorite books or movies or games that you can revisit again and again? All the things that you feel excited about and all the characters that you are picturing—whatever you're imagining right now, you're a fan of it. And, good news, you can be a fan of anything and everything, and you can be a fan of more than one thing, too. There are fantasy fans, video game fans, sports team fans, and so many more.

A fan is a person who has a strong interest or admiration for a particular person or thing.

The best thing about being a fan is that you'll be connected with others through a mutual passion for any given story or character, which also means that you don't have to hide your interests. Be loud and proud, and don't even think twice about whether you should get that backpack with a design from your favorite manga on it. Talk about your favorite characters and the stories you like with your friends and family—even tell your teachers. Another wonderful thing about being a fan is that you're part of a fandom—a community of people who are fans of the same things as you and understand exactly why those things are important to you. Tons of other people share the same passions as you; you'll belong to a number of found families across the globe. Just like there are no limits on how many things you can love and enjoy, there are absolutely no limits on how many fandoms you can join. You might find one fandom to pour your entire heart into, or you might participate in many of them.

Fandom is a community of people who are fans of someone or something.

It's easy to be part of fandom, too. The main thing—really the only thing—you have to bring to the party is love. That's what being a fan is all about. It's caring so much about a story that you keep thinking about it long after the story ends. It's appreciating the worlds and characters others have created; it's celebrating them from a place of love and kindness. Keep those warm and fuzzy feelings in mind as you explore the world of fandom, and you can't go wrong.

As a fan that is new to the community, you might have a lot of questions like: How can I express myself in my fandom or share it with friends? How can I build communities and find other fans to gush with over my favorite fictional stories? How can I attend that convention I've been hearing about?

Well, one way is to read this book. Inside, you'll find information on how to get started exploring different types of fandoms and communities, tips, tricks, and even advice from fans who have made fandom part of their careers! You can read this book cover to cover or jump in and read the chapters in any order, because, like fandom, this book is flexible. We even have a handy quiz to help you decide what kind of community might interest you the most and where to begin on your journey on page 5.

It took me a while to discover what fandom is and how I fit in, but once I did, I felt like I could be myself. My hope is that this book will help you find your footing as a fan and learn how to get more involved than ever in your fandom.

May the Force be with you,

Amy Ratcliffe

What Kind of Fan Are You?

ARE YOU READY TO GET morc creative with your fandom and express yourself? Take this quiz to find a place to start your journey. Circle whichever answers feel best for you right now, and don't worry if you're having trouble deciding. You can totally choose more than one answer for each question if you want.

In your free time, you're most likely to do which of these things?

a. Finish a craft project you've been working on.

b. Cozy up with a good book.

c. Chat with your friends about a cool new thing you learned.

d. Organize an outing with friends to see a movie.

e. Beat the next level of your video game.

f. Open your sketch pad and draw.

How do you share your fandom with friends?

a. We coordinate matching outfits or accessories based on our favorite characters.

b. We come up with stories about our most loved fictional worlds.

c. We debate our favorite fan theories.

d. We plan watch parties for the shows and movies we enjoy.

e. We explore online realms together.

f. We draw our favorite characters and create new ones.

What excites you most about your fandom?

a. The elaborate costumes.

b. All the world-building details.

c. Learning new things about the characters or world.

d. Being able to share and enjoy it with my friends.

e. Being able to play a role in the story.

f. The design and look of the characters and backgrounds.

When you watch the latest episode of your favorite TV series, which of these things are you most likely to say to a friend about it?

a. "Did you see that costume at the end? I need it."

b. "I liked it, but the book is better."

c. "Can we please pick this apart at lunch tomorrow?"

d. "Wait, let me start a group chat about all of this, because we need everyone to weigh in."

e. "They didn't explain the rules for using time travel!"

f. "That spooky mansion is gorgeous. I can't get over the design!"

Your favorite class in school is:

    a. Industrial arts

    b. Creative writing

    c. Debate

    d. Theater

    e. Programming

    f. Art

Count how many of each letter you circled and get a clue about how you may want to express your fandom—but remember, you can ultimately choose any of these you want!

    a. Courageous Cosplayer

    b. Fantastic Fanfic Writer

    c. Prestigious Podcaster

    d. Canny Community Builder

    e. Gutsy Gamer

    f. Fabulous Fan Artist

CHAPTER ONE

Pen and Paper

ONE WAY TO CELEBRATE THE things you love is to create stories or art based on them. Taking elements of the shows, characters, games, and other things you like and including them in stories or art that you create is known as making fan fiction and fanart, respectively. These are two different ways you can reimagine some of your favorite stories and characters and put your own stamp on them, including doing so through fanzines and webcomics. Fanfic and fanart in their many forms have been around since the 1950s, and the labels were coined shortly thereafter as a way to help differentiate fan-created materials from officially authorized releases.

Fanfic, fanart, zines, and webcomics started out with people sharing stories and illustrations in smaller, private groups, but now they're all well-known, mainstream practices with creators and fans connecting from all over the world. (Yep, you can even be a fan of a fan-created work, too.)

When something is mainstream, it is widely known and accepted by not only fans but people outside of the fandom's community.

■ ■ ■ ■

An underground work is generally seen as more experimental and as an alternative to more well-known, popular things and is known by a smaller group of fans or specific audiences.

Some of your favorite creators got their start by making their own versions of the things they love. Artists who have posted their fanart on social media have worked on some very cool official projects. Erin Lefler put her illustrations on Instagram, and now she contributes designs to Lucasfilm for *Star Wars* merchandise. (You can learn more about her journey and read her advice in the Artist Spotlight on page 17.) Writers who have shared their fanfic online for years garner invested readers and sometimes go on to work on licensed books and stories. Many of your favorite published authors have also written fanfic, like Neil Gaiman, for example, who used to write *Chronicles of Narnia* fanfic. Even the Hugo Awards, which are literary awards given each year for the best works of science fiction or fantasy, have awards for Best Fan Artist and Best Fan Writer.

Regardless of whether you go on to produce official work for the stories you love or not, the most important and wonderful thing about making your own fanfic and fanart is being able to showcase your imagination and creativity while sharpening your storytelling and illustrating skills. By beginning to write or draw using a cherished fictional world, you are stretching your writer and artist legs in familiar territory.

You can work in a world or with characters that you already are very comfortable with and give yourself permission to explore and be creative without the stress of creating a new world from scratch. And the more you put your creative mind to work, even if you're using existing characters and settings, the more you strengthen it, and these skills will come in handy when you want to write or draw your own characters. Fanfic and fanart also open the door to important explorations of relationships and stories that the existing media and canon may not portray. It's all about making the story uniquely yours.

The canon is the source material for the fictional universe you adore. It's material that's officially part of the story. Canon can be closed (when all the material is completed) or open (when material isn't finished or released yet).

Fan Fiction

Fan fiction is fan-written text, usually prose, starring characters and places from existing movies, TV series, games, or books. The world of fanfic is vast and has many different communities with fans of all kinds and from around the world, contributing stories online in forums, webcomics, and fanzines. While fanfic has a very long history, the medium grew in popularity and developed into what it is today because a group of amazing female *Star Trek* fans wanted to write about Captain Kirk and Spock's adventures, usually romantic ones, in the 1970s. Because of these early zines, conventions, message boards, electronic mailing lists, and search archives, and all the fanfic that was available there, fandom—and fan-created work—has grown into what it is today. For example, take Archive of Our Own, or AO3 for short. As of this writing, AO3 has over five million works of fan fiction. Five. Million. That's a lot of stories.

But how to even start imagining your own fanfic? Well, picture the sparkling shores of Cerulean City in *Pokémon* or imagine the fireplace crackling softly in a quiet hobbit hole in *Lord of the Rings*' Middle-earth. Think about *Sailor Moon*'s Usagi Tsukino or maybe Bow from *She-Ra and the Princesses of Power*. You can use those settings, or those characters, or any others you want in a story *you* write. If you can think of a fandom, fans are probably writing fanfic for it. But don't let that stop you from telling your own transformative works based on the canon of your fandom. Maybe one of the universes you love has made you think, *But what if a certain character chose a different path? What would that look like?* You can write exactly what it would look like. Think about what you want the characters to do and what you want them to feel. You are in control, and you are free to dream up your favorite places and characters in new stories—your stories.

This also means that you can write at your own pace and in your own way. It's okay to start small or try something new—don't feel like you have to commit to writing a novel. Begin with a drabble, which is a short piece of fiction that's one hundred words, and don't worry, it's okay if you go a bit over.

The blank page can be intimidating, and you might find yourself starting to have doubts. What will you fill it with? What if it's not the most amazing story ever? I get it. The best advice, however, is to dive on in. The water will be fine. It's all an exercise in creativity. Some writing prompts might help you conceptualize like: Character A invites Character B on a vacation. Where will they go? What will the packing process be like? What sights will they see? Or imagine your characters have to learn to defend themselves from supernatural beings. How do they prepare? Who do they ask to help them train?

Just swap in whichever characters you want and get writing! When you're finished, it's time to share your work with your family and friends who participate in your fandom.

WRITER SPOTLIGHT

ALAN GRATZ

Alan Gratz writes novels for young readers,
including *Samurai Shortstop* and *The Brooklyn Nine*.

What was your first fandom?

Star Wars was my first real intensive fan experience. I was five years old when the very first *Star Wars* movie came out. I loved the grand scope of it. In particular, I loved that it felt like a real universe that was lived in. Equipment was junky and worn. Robots got different-colored parts put on them when they broke. People rode around on lots of different kinds of animals and ate different kinds of food. And the movies never felt the need to explain all of that. That information was filled in with the expanded universe of comics and books and toys, but it really let fans of the movies fill in the blanks of that world. I think that's a key to fandom—there's a sandbox there with lots of cool toys to play with, but how you play with them and what you make of it is up to you.

Did you use your *Star Wars* fandom to write fanfic?

When I'd come home, I would go out in the backyard and pretend to be Han Solo or Luke Skywalker and have adventures. But I wasn't reliving the movies—I was making up new stories based on those characters and that world. I had a bunch of the action figures, too, and would make up elaborate stories with those. What I was really doing was creating fan fiction. There wasn't a word for it then, or if there was, I had never heard it. Creating stories in the *Star Wars* universe was fun and easy, and that eventually led to me creating my own characters and my own worlds as an author.

What advice would you give to a kid who wants to start writing fanfic?

Go for it! Dive in! Don't worry about getting published, though. Not yet. Share your stuff with other fans. There's a real joy in finding and connecting with that one other person out there as passionate about your fandom as you are. I also love taking secondary and tertiary characters and building up a life and adventures for them. My favorite *Star Wars* action figure when I was a kid was Bespin Guard. He had a mustache and wore a cool blue suit and hat. He didn't have a name, though. I loved him because I could make up his name and his story. He was a complete blank slate, and yet he existed in this incredibly rich, wonderful world I loved. He became the main character in my stories, with the more famous characters—Luke, Han, Leia, Chewie, the droids—as *his* secondary characters.

Any artist who creates art based on a work they don't own is making fanart. Every person's artistic style is special and individual, so one artist's drawing of the TARDIS from *Doctor Who* won't be like anyone else's. The concept or object or character may come from an existing canon, but a nifty thing about fanart is that the artist can make those things come to life in a way that no one else can. The term *art* in fanart broadly applies to digital or traditional drawings and paintings, but can also include things like animated gifs, photo manipulations, text-heavy images, sculptures, fiber work, or graphic designs. Fanart is flexible and includes many different styles, just like fanfic, but captured in a more visual medium.

Nothing is off-limits in fanart, and many artists find inspiration from all kinds of their favorite pop culture stories and mediums—from books to films, video games, and so much more. Fanart is all about being creative and showing the world how you see your beloved characters and places. Artistic license is encouraged. If you are inspired by your favorite book, you can illustrate a character or a location based on their descriptions and how you imagine them to look.

The same goes for creating art of a place or character you've seen on the screen as well. You don't have to draw Naruto just the way he is depicted in the manga, for instance, or draw Lara Croft exactly the way you see her in *Tomb Raider* movies or in the video games—unless you want to. Artists often have particular illustration styles, so they'll pose a character in a way that best showcases their signature style.

If you like to draw, chances are you've already doodled your fandoms in the margins of your notebooks. That's a wonderful way to start making fanart. To further practice your skills, try drawing one character or place a week. Choose a fandom that speaks to your heart and draw anything from a custom *Mario Kart* track to your take on Ursula from *The Little Mermaid*.

HISTORY LESSON: ARTIST TRADING CARDS

One way to make and collect art is with artist trading cards (known as ATCs). These are mini pieces of art, sized 2.5 inches by 3.5 inches (or 63 millimeters by 89 millimeters) that can fit inside card collector sheets. The small size means they're fun to make and don't take up a ton of room. It's a wonderful way to build up a collection of original work from your favorite artists.

And ATCs are relatively new, too. The movement started when a Swiss artist named M. Vänçi Stirnemann made 1,200 of these little cards by hand for an exhibit in 1997. When his exhibit ended, he asked others to make art cards and trade with him. The recently formed tradition continues today as people meet up for ATC swaps at conventions or local events. It's made the jump to digital, too, as you can either coordinate swaps of physical cards by mail or make entirely digital cards to share with someone.

Art supply stores carry drawing pads sized specifically for ATCs, but you don't have to limit yourself to paper. As long as your creation is small enough to fit in a collector sleeve, you can make it from any medium, like fiber or a collage of found objects.

—— ARTIST SPOTLIGHT ——
ERIN LEFLER

Erin Lefler is a character designer, concept artist,
and licensed Lucasfilm and Marvel merchandise artist.

When did you become interested in being an artist, and did any particular fandoms inspire you?

I've been interested in art ever since I could pick up a pencil. I would drive my parents insane as a child trying to draw all over everything I could get my hands on! I was definitely interested in drawing *Star Wars* growing up, but also Marvel Comics, because I was an avid comic book reader. I adored Spider-Man.

How did sharing fanart online help you get professional work?

I had been working as a freelancer for a couple of years before I was encouraged to put my work online. I love making fanart when I'm not making art for work, so I just started posting the art I made of the things I loved, and people started following my work, which, for me, was insane. I had put my application into a lot of different places about a year after starting my social media accounts and got a lot of rejections. But I ended up getting an e-mail from Lucasfilm, and I remember them saying, "We've seen your work online and we love what we see." So I feel it's a very important thing to put your work out on social media.

What advice would you give to kids who want to celebrate their fandom by making art?

Do it. I can't stress it enough—don't let anything or anyone stop you. If it's what you love and you want to express it by making art, cosplaying, writing, and so on, do it. You'll find some people along the way who love the same things as you. You'll be able to make some cool art, and who knows—maybe someday you'll be able to take that and make a career out of it like I got to!

Webcomics

If you have a fondness for both fanfic and fanart, you might want to think about combining the two and making a webcomic. It's a way to tell stories visually through panels of art and words—like comic books for the web! Usually released in brief installments on a regular schedule, webcomics can use existing fandoms and canons as a base for their stories or feature completely new, original content. The history of webcomics goes way back to the '80s, but they became more popular in the mid-1990s because of how much easier it was to create and share work on the internet.

Then, the medium had another big spike in South Korea in the 2000s, with the help of the webcomics platform LINE Webtoon, also known as just Webtoon outside of Korea. Today, you can easily read webcomics on your phone or computer through platforms like Tapas, Webtoon, Tappytoon, The Duck Webcomics, and more—even on Instagram and Imgur. With so many new creators writing and drawing amazing stories now, some companies are even adapting webcomics into physical comics and graphic novels, like *Check, Please* and *Heartstopper*, or into animated series and anime, such as *Lore Olympus* and *Tower of God*.

Of course, if you only want to write or draw and not do both, then webcomics are also ideal for collaboration. Plus, making a webcomic with a friend might help you come up with even better ideas and learn how to cooperatively tell a story. Two heads are better than one, you know. If making a webcomic sounds like a blast, the next thing you should do is focus on the type of story or characters that you want your comic to have. Don't worry too much about the audience or what is popular right now. Instead, create a story based on whichever of your fandoms inspires you, like an animated series you can't get enough of or the latest superhero movie that blew your socks off. If you are working with a friend, talk about the different things you both love—and maybe a few of the things that you don't—so that you can gather all the elements that you want in your webcomic.

The next stage is to throw it all down on paper and see what magic happens. Sketch out thumbnails, which are rough representations of what you want the comic panel to look like, and write ideas for dialogue underneath them. Thumbnails will give you an excellent starting place to organize your thoughts and refine your art before you go on to your final illustrations, dialogue, and story. Maybe you'll find that your story needs a few installments to complete; if so, you can sketch those out, too.

Remember, there's no single way to create a webcomic, so experiment and see what works best for you and the stories you want to tell. Then, with the help of older family members, you can upload your drawing to the web. If you're making digital art, make a template to unify the look of all your installments, and start illustrating. Don't forget to come up with a name for your new webcomic and, most importantly, be sure to sign your work—be proud of what you've made!

FANDOM MATH
WEBCOMICS + CONVENTIONS

Been working on a webcomic and headed to a convention soon? This is the perfect time to share your webcomic—either the finished version or just your ideas—with people you meet. If you have panels already done, save them on a mobile device and take it with you to the convention. Or get help making bookmarks or postcards with your work. Then give them to anyone you'd like at the convention, perhaps to other fans you meet or to exhibiting artists.

— ARTIST SPOTLIGHT —

JEN BARTEL

Jen Bartel is an Eisner Award–winning illustrator and comic artist.
She's done work for Marvel, Disney, Adidas, and more.

What was your first fandom?

My first fandom was probably *Sailor Moon*, which functioned on a very local level in that there were so many young girls when I was in elementary school who were really into *SM*, and it helped us build friendships. We spent a lot of time creating our own Sailor Senshi OCs [original characters] and trading our treasured *SM* stickers and books with each other. The first fandom I participated in on a larger scale was *Final Fantasy VII*, though. By this point, I was in high school, and internet forums were booming with fanart and fan fiction. Finding my people was much easier within fandom spaces, and I'll always be thankful for that!

When did you become interested in being an artist?

Even when I was a child, there was very little question about what I wanted to be— it was always "artist," but I hadn't quite nailed down the specific type of artist. Honestly, I've always been a fan of lots of different pop culture properties, but it wasn't until I was in my midtwenties and my nephews were born that I started realizing how much of a positive impact media could have on kids and how much of an effect it had had on me personally. That's what made me want to get into working on major properties in a professional capacity. So many of us are shaped by stories about superheroes and magical girls, and while they might seem fleeting or silly, in my mind, these stories really are equivalent to modern-day mythology.

What does it mean to you that you get to make art your career?

I feel so incredibly lucky to be able to do what I love for a living. While I don't agree with the idea that "doing what you love means you won't ever work a day in your life," and I definitely recognize it as work that is deserving of fair pay, it still feels quite surreal most days to be able to draw full-time, especially because I spent so many years after graduating from college working retail and service jobs, thinking I would only have nights and weekends for drawing.

What advice would you give to kids who want to celebrate their fandom by making art?

Don't be afraid to get creative and run with your ideas, and don't let anyone make you feel ashamed for being passionate about something. Have as much fun with it as you can, and share it with others as much as possible!

Fanzines

As much as you adore your favorite movies, books, video games, and other things, you might feel like the companies making them may not offer the kind of supplemental material you want, and fanzines are an inventive way to fill that gap. Say you want to read all you can and learn more about the world of *Jurassic Park* and would love to see maps of the various islands from the different films, scientific dinosaur information, and an essay about how amazing Dr. Ellie Sattler is. If this dino publication of your dreams doesn't exist, then you can step in and make it yourself. You have the power to create what's called a *fanzine*, or a fan-made magazine. Even if there is a magazine about *Jurassic Park*, you can, and should, still make your own version because you're making it with your own passions, perspective, and ideas, which is what will make it unique.

Fanzines are different from fanfic because instead of telling a single fictional story, zines are very similar to real magazines and can encompass a wide variety of things. Fanzines can have short stories, art, editorial articles, interviews, or essays. In short, you can make your fanzine whatever you want it to be, and you can add your own fan creations into your zine or include your friends' work. Go ahead and brainstorm what you'd like to explore or learn more about for one of your fandoms. Then ask yourself, if you could pick up a magazine all about that fandom, what would you hope to see in it? Write down your answers in a list, name yourself editor in chief of your publication, and ask friends who share your fandom to contribute articles, poems, comic strips, art, or other materials. Don't be afraid to think outside of the box! You could make some faux in-universe advertisements like Wookiee shampoo if it's a *Star Wars* zine or dino spray for a *Jurassic Park* zine.

HISTORY LESSON: RIOT GRRRL ZINES

The idea of modern fanzines goes back to *The Comet*, a science fiction magazine published in 1930, but zines didn't stop at focusing on sci-fi or other fictional universes. In the early 1990s, zines played a huge role in Riot Grrrl, an underground feminist movement connecting women in the punk music scene.

During a time when over forty thousand zines were published in North America, Riot Grrrl zines found avid readers since zines were easy to make and distribute and also because these zines spoke to a previously unexplored fandom niche. The publications connected countless people across the United States in pushing back against sexism in punk culture. Other Riot Grrrl zines such as *Jigsaw* (founded by a member of the band Bikini Kill), *Snarla*, and *Manifixation* featured everything from interviews with musicians to literary essays to DIY projects, and found a network of subscribers.

The creators of these zines didn't see the kind of publications and conversations they wanted to in the world around them, so they decided to start them as a way to share their thoughts and passion with others. You can do the same with the things that you love as well.

Once you've collected all the stories, art, quizzes, essays, comics, and materials you want in your fanzine, it's time to publish it. There are two main types of zines, digital or physical, and you'll have to decide if you want to publish your fanzine online or go a more traditional, paper-focused route.

To create a physical fanzine, you'll need access to a copy machine or printer and a stapler. Don't worry about the length of your fanzine, and do whatever feels right. When you have all the submissions, apply your arts-and-crafts know-how to cut and paste everything onto standard-size pieces of paper in whatever order you want. Don't forget to add design elements and a cover—made by you or a friend. Once you've brought the fanzine together with your mad talents, make copies using the copy machine or printer, staple the pages together, and then distribute them. Do it for free or ask for a few cents each just to cover any printing and copy costs you incurred. This pretty much makes you a publisher now, so remember to put that on your résumé.

If you aren't interested in the paper route or want to use a computer to help you assemble your zine, you can adapt this process to be entirely digital. Collect all the stories, essays, and other text materials into a word-processing document and, with the help of an older family member, use photo editing programs like GIMP or Canva to arrange your submissions into a beautiful fanzine. Then you can print the finished product or share it with the world through e-mail or online with your parent or guardian's permission.

Finally, it's worth noting that fan creations are just that: creations made by fans. Copyright holders for various intellectual properties (such as *My Little Pony* or *Stranger Things*) claim ownership over the characters and stories associated with the property, and they typically do not consider fanfic and fanart to be negative—especially if the fans aren't selling their work. However, it's always best to be clear that your creations are not official when sharing online or with the fandom community. Remember you're playing in someone else's sandbox, so always be respectful of the copyright holder's rules. And be kind when enjoying another fan's or creator's work!

MAKING-IT-HAPPEN TOOL KIT

Writing and making art only requires having a handful of items in your tool kit. If you want to use more high-grade or specialized supplies, prioritize what materials and tools you want, and talk to an older family member about making a savings plan so you can buy them. Here are some basics that are good to always have on hand:

Pen • Pencil • Lined notebook • Colored pencils • Brushes with paints • Artist drawing pads (Tip: The type of paper you use will depend on what type of method you are doing—ink versus watercolor, etc.) • Computer with word processing software or free digital art software • Printer

— WRITER SPOTLIGHT —
DANIEL JOSÉ OLDER

Daniel José Older is the *New York Times* best-selling author of *Dactyl Hill Squad* and the *Shadowshaper Cypher* series.

What was your first fandom?

My first fandom was actually *Star Wars*. I saw *Return of the Jedi* when I was three years old. It was my first movie in a movie theater, and I remember it very clearly because the rancor scared me so much I had to run out of the theater in tears. But then I ran right back in, and then I kept going back again and again even though the movie was terrifying. I just loved it.

Is there a particular story that made you want to create?

Star Wars is definitely one of the foundations. Greek mythology is another and then expanded into all mythology for sure. *The Iliad* was one of my favorite books when I was younger. Then politics in general. It's the whole span. It's really the intersection or the crossroads of history and mythology and sci-fi and politics and all that stuff.

What advice would you give to a kid who wants to start writing?

Tell the story that you want to tell. Don't try to fit it into a box. Just tell that story that you're dying to tell. Yeah, maybe you'll be using characters that you know from other worlds, but don't let that make you feel like you have to turn it into something that you don't totally believe in. Find your voice and enjoy it. Go wild on the page with things that you've never ever seen, because that's what you want to see. That's why we write, to create worlds that we want to see but haven't yet.

Fan fiction is so important, especially right now. I think it's such an amazing opportunity for people to envision themselves and their friends and their family members in these worlds that don't always show them that. That's why fan fiction exists, in part.

READY PLAYER TWO

After you put in all the work to channel your beautiful passion for your fandom into your fan creations, you'll want to show them off. And that's excellent, because others want to see it. One way to showcase your work is to share it with family members and friends. Hand out hard copies or call them over to the computer to read your stories and zines or enjoy your art and webcomics. These trusted members of your inner circle will provide helpful feedback if you ask for their thoughts. Remember, they're giving you their thoughts to help you improve, so try to listen to their critiques with an open mind.

Another avenue to share your work is to put your creations online. Instagram and Tumblr are sweet spots to share fanart, while places like Archive of Our Own (AO3) are designed specifically for fan fiction. Ask an older family member to help you open an account and make your first posts. Be sure to check with them anytime you want to log in and read comments, participate in discussions, or add your latest pieces to your account.

As you explore the world of fan creations, you might come across some words, phrases, or other things that you don't know. Good news, we have a handy glossary on page 125 that will help you navigate this cool new world.

CHAPTER TWO

Playing the Part

COSPLAY EQUALS COSTUME PLUS PLAY. A Japanese magazine first coined this version of the word in the early 1980s, and just like the equation says, cosplaying is when you wear a costume and pretend to be a fictional character. If you've ever put on a costume for Halloween or pulled outfits out of a trunk and pretended to be someone (or something) else, then congratulations, you've already cosplayed.

While the word *cosplay* is relatively new, people have worn costumes for hundreds of years. Think about it: actors put on costumes for roles in theater productions, and other times, people played dress-up for fun. Performers in Kabuki, a Japanese dance-drama dating back to the 1600s, wore elaborate makeup called kumadori, while masks and elaborate costumes were all the rage for masquerade balls, which go back to the fifteenth century during Carnival festivities in Italy. Part of the fun was disguising yourself and seeing if anyone you knew could recognize you. That aspect of masked balls and makeup is still true for

Halloween today. Isn't it fun when your own neighbors and friends don't know who you are beneath your Halloween costume?

Cosplay is so exciting and fun because it builds upon the foundation of costuming's lengthy history while also offering people of all kinds the ability to dress up and be who, or what, ever they want to be. Fan cosplay itself has some cool background under its belt, too. The world's first science fiction convention in 1939, Worldcon I, hosted the first-ever recorded fan costume—a couple who made ensembles inspired by the covers of sci-fi magazines. Myrtle Douglas's and Forrest Ackerman's outfits gave other fans the idea that dressing up was cool, so future conventions, including the very next Worldcon, saw others don costumes based on their favorite characters.

Cosplay comes back to celebrating your fandom from a place of love and enthusiasm. Creating an outfit and cosplaying as a character you adore is an excellent way to express your fandom and share your love with the community. You'll have to tap into that passion as you build your costume, because cosplay, like all the other activities in this book, takes time, patience, practice, and hard work—but it's rewarding work. Designing and building a costume will help you stretch your crafting muscles in ways you might not have anticipated, so don't get discouraged if you have to learn new skills to create your perfect cosplay.

Then, once you've finished it, don't be afraid to show it off! You can wear your finished costume to many places, so don't let the fear of it sitting in your closet deter you from creating. Put on your costume for a convention, for Halloween, for a costume party, for a photo shoot at home, or plan a costume sleepover with your friends and encourage them to bring their costumes, too! Heck, you can wear it to the grocery store as long as you get the okay from your parents or guardians.

Getting Started

First things first, who do you want to cosplay as? Make a list of five characters you love and that you want to dress like. They can be from any fictional universe, the page or the screen, or any gender. Think big and be bold! Do your favorite characters wear ball gowns, or a tank top and jeans, or armor? Pull together pictures of the character you're dressing up as, reference images, or your own doodles to help guide your way.

Gender-bending, also known as Rule 63, is when we imagine a character as a different gender. For example, if a cosplayer imagined Elsa from *Frozen* as a male character, then maybe they would wear a striking royal suit with a cape instead of a frosty blue dress.

Now choose one character from your list. Think about the clothes and shoes they wear and any props or accessories they use. Depending on the type and style of cosplay that you're working on, it might help to break the outfit into different components to help you get started. Create a schedule to stay on track. Start a cosplay journal where you can keep all your thoughts, ideas, sketches, references, and notes about different costumes that you want to make and have made—don't forget to add photos of you wearing your finished cosplays. Look up reference images from the source material, a.k.a. the canon, or ask an adult to help you look for some online.

While you're online, see if anyone else has made this costume before; if so, maybe they've posted useful information and guides you can apply to your project. Other cosplayers are always happy to share advice about their handiwork, so ask lots of questions. Check out books from your local library about crafting, sewing, or costume design to help you plan out how to start your project. Research your character—watch movies, play games, or look at fanart and official art—to inspire you and use for references images and sketches, too. As you start to plan your cosplay, break down every element of the character's look and outfit from head to toe—like a brown hat, long blond hair, a blue vest, a gray T-shirt, a dagger, and so on. Be sure to include all the character's distinguishing features and accessories.

Before heading to the craft or thrift store, think about what clothes you might have in your closet that you can use, then decide what you need or want to craft and what you might want to buy. If you need to make something, check your tool kit first (see page 42), then list all the extra or specialty supplies you'll need in your journal. For instance, you might want to use a specific type of craft foam for armor or a certain pattern and fabric for a cloak or a dress. As you acquire or make different pieces of your cosplay, check them off your master list, so you can keep track of your progress. Making a costume can take time, and you may have to chip away at this project bit by bit for a little while, but when you're done, you'll have a rad cosplay to rock and show off.

AKAKIOGA COSPLAY

Akakioga Cosplay cosplays at a number
of conventions and is a Stars of Cosplay model.

What was your first fandom?

I was super deep into *Inuyasha*! Funny enough, my mom and I both watched it when I was a kid, which is probably why it holds such fun memories for me. I also watched *Pokémon*, *Digimon*, and all those fun Saturday morning cartoons. But *Inuyasha* still holds such a special place in my heart for some reason. Between the colorful cast of characters, to the epic fight scenes, it was all around a fun show to watch!

What inspired you to craft your first costume, and what was it?

My first costume I made from scratch was Kiki from *Kiki's Delivery Service*. It was a simple dress pattern that really sparked my drive to start making my own stuff. From there, I continued making easy costumes until I felt comfortable tackling harder designs.

When you know you want to make a certain costume, what are the next steps? How do you plan?

Typically, when I am dead set on making a costume, I'll go into research mode. I'll begin looking at reference images of the character, begin gathering fabric/material ideas online, and go from there. If it's a complex build, I'll even sketch out pieces on paper to help me break it down into simpler ideas before building it. Sometimes the planning process can take longer than building the costume because I really try to make sure I'm 100 percent ready to begin.

What advice would you give to kids who want to try cosplay?

Cosplay is and should always be for fun! No matter what you look like, what walk of life you come from, what fandoms you're part of, you will always be welcomed into our community. Pick a character you really love and go for it. There is no right or wrong way to cosplay. So, no matter if you buy it or make it yourself, as long as you have fun with it, that's all that matters.

Cosplay Types

One of the great things about cosplay is that there are so many ways to do it, you can go big or small, elaborate or minimal, and anywhere in between. Like with other fan creations, don't feel like you have to be an expert right away, and make sure you start at a pace that is comfortable for you. To help you decide where you might want to start, let's review some of the different types of cosplay that you can create to help spark some ideas.

REPLICA COSPLAY

If you want to make and wear an exact replica of Miles Morales's black-and-red Spider-Man suit, you can absolutely do that. Making costumes exactly like the ones you've seen on-screen or in the pages of a comic book will take time, hard work, help from grown-ups, and patience, but it is totally possible. Many cosplayers make these kinds of costumes with gorgeous results. Take a look at their creations and tutorials and tons of screen captures or reference pictures of the costume you want to duplicate.

CASUAL COSPLAY

So maybe you're not ready to construct a full-blown mech suit yet, but don't worry, because lots of characters wear more casual outfits and everyday clothes like jeans and T-shirts. Casual or closet cosplay is cosplay that you put together with clothes you already own and is a great way to get started and gain experience designing cosplay outfits. Look in your closet, do you have a pair of denim overalls and a green shirt? Congratulations, now you're Luigi from *Super Mario Bros*. What about gray pants, a cream-colored shirt, and a brown jacket? Awesome, now you have the same outfit that Finn wears in *Star Wars*. A blue dress, red shoes, and a red hair ribbon? Ta-da, grab a broom, because you're Kiki from *Kiki's Delivery Service*. Without even having to sit down at a sewing machine, you can become a plumber, a rebel hero, a witch, and so much more.

With casual cosplay, all your skirts, sweatshirts, T-shirts, and jeans are costume materials. Look through your closet and drawers with that in mind—don't forget to check your shoes and accessories! Make an inventory list and take notes in your cosplay journal about the basics of what you own and in what colors. Check your cosplay inspiration board and see if there are any outfits that you can try to make with what you already have. You'll probably come up with at least three cosplay outfits just from a first look.

HISTORY LESSON: DISNEYBOUNDING

Believe it or not, this is a kind of casual cosplay created specifically for Disney fans. Leslie Kay came up with the term in 2011 when she was bound to Walt Disney World for a vacation. When planning and deciding what to wear on her trip, she started making lookbooks online featuring modern outfits inspired by the classic costumes of different Disney characters. (Tip: Lookbooks can be an excellent place to start when thinking about and planning a casual cosplay.)

DisneyBounding doesn't involve wearing wigs or carrying elaborate props like other cosplay types; instead, it's all about color blocking and using accessories like jewelry or bags to mimic the look of a certain Disney character.

For example, instead of painting your skin blue and wearing a mask to look like the Genie from *Aladdin*, you could do a DisneyBound option by pairing a blue dress—or a blue top and pants—with a bold red belt. Adding extra accessories like gold colored bracelets to represent the Genie's cuffs or wearing magic lamp earrings or a necklace make for the perfect finishing touches.

When you mix-and-match outfit components based on their solid colors, this is known as color blocking. In casual or DisneyBound cosplay, this technique is used by wearing everyday clothes that match the color, style, or patterns of your favorite characters' outfits.

GROUP COSPLAY

While you're going through your everyday clothes, maybe you'll find the perfect pink dress and tights for a Princess Bubblegum cosplay and remember that a friend has a plaid shirt that is a perfect match for Marceline from *Adventure Time.* This would be the perfect opportunity for a group cosplay. Group cosplay is just what it sounds like: a group of people picking out characters from the same story or universe to cosplay as together. If you and your friends are part of the same fandoms, then it can be really easy and fun to coordinate a group cosplay. You can cosplay together as those characters at a convention, a party, for a photo shoot, or whenever you want to wear your costumes, which is a perfectly valid and magnificent reason.

Since you're cosplaying as part of a group, teamwork and communication are very important. Be sure to listen to everyone's ideas and that your group agrees on what type of cosplay you are doing. Like creating cosplay for yourself, remember that your group can choose detailed and complex costumes or go for more casual versions. For example, you can go all out as Disney princesses or look to *Ralph Breaks the Internet* for a more casual, laid-back approach to princess cosplay.

Remember, group cosplay is all about having fun creating, working on, and showing off your costumes together. Once your group has figured out when and where you're going to wear your fantastic creations, try planning cosplay-making parties or times when you all can meet up for a few hours to pool supplies and tools. Don't forget that working as a team means that you should all be willing to give each other advice and support and maybe even lend and borrow outfit pieces or accessories as well.

COSPLAY HELPERS

If one of your friends or someone in the group—maybe even you—likes the idea of cosplay but doesn't want to wear a costume, they can still be involved in this cool, creative hobby. One way to do this is by exploring some of the several important supporting roles that exist in the cosplay community. Even professional cosplayers have friends in supporting roles who help them with everything from crafting, to putting on wigs, to posing for photos. Plus, if you're interested in cosplay, but still not entirely sure if it is for you, this is a perfect way to surround yourself with cosplay and learn about the ins-and-outs of the community. Let's learn about cosplay support roles you can try.

Be a cosmaker. If you enjoy sewing, painting, or putting things together, maybe you can become the costume-making expert for your group and make costumes for your friends. Flex your skills and your curiosity to help craft gorgeous outfits, and teach others how to do what you do.

Be a helper. Costumes can be elaborate and a lot of work for one person to put on by themselves. You can offer a hand to friends at conventions by doing things like assisting with putting on armor, securing a wig, or carrying a bag with essentials like water and regular clothes—they'll really appreciate the helping hand.

Be a medic. Some coshelpers make being a cosplay medic their whole role at conventions. They walk around or set up small booths with everything they might need to fix any snags or loose parts that cosplayers need help addressing. Feel free to dress up or create a sign—some medics carry fun shields—and have little cosplay repair kit with double-sided tape, safety pins, fabric glue, a needle and thread, and other materials on hand to help out.

Be a photographer. Cosplayers work hard to create amazing outfits, and they usually want their costumes to be seen and recorded. You can capture all their looks as a cosplay photographer and take pictures with your mobile device, a digital camera, or even a camera with instant film. Try to find unique public places at conventions with fun backdrops. For example, step outside the exhibit hall and see if the lobby has any interesting walls or windows—things that would provide a superior background to a bunch of convention attendees in a crowded aisle. Remember, cosplay doesn't equal consent, so always ask permission before you take a photo of someone, and don't forget to have some cards on hand that tell cosplayers your name and where they can find your photos.

READY PLAYER TWO

Creating one-of-a-kind outfits is a fun challenge, but even professionals need an assistant. When working with crafting tools, make sure you have an older family member show you how to safely use tools like hot glue guns, sewing machines, and crafting knives. Not only can they help you measure fabric or model your works in progress, but they'll be excited to help you bring your costume to life, too.

MAKING-IT-HAPPEN TOOL KIT

You'll need different materials for each cosplay project, but you'll use a few kinds of things again and again, so it's a good idea to keep a tool kit of these basic items on hand. Check with adults to see if you have any of these items at home first before buying. Otherwise, you can find these items at local craft or hardware stores and online.

Pencils, colored pencils, or markers • Paper or journal • White chalk • Scissors • Ruler or measuring tape • Pins • Sewing needles and thread • Fabric tape or fusible webbing • Hot glue gun and glue • Strips of Velcro

FANDOM MATH
COSPLAY + PODCASTING

If you're into making costumes and you also want to try creating a podcast, why not make your podcast about your cosplay adventures? Share how you got into cosplay and what you like about it. Episode topics could include tips for crafting foam props, interviews with other cosplayers, or even advice on how to research a costume and get started.

PHILIP ODANGO OF CANVAS COSPLAY

Philip Odango of Canvas Cosplay is a professional cosplayer and author of the Cosplay Professional Development Series.

What was your first fandom, and what about it resonated with you?

My first fandom was *Mighty Morphin Power Rangers*. As a youngling, I, too, was a teen-ager with an attitude. The series had all the elements of escapism—a hero's quest, magical transformations, dinosaur robots, monsters made out of clay that grew into giants, and a pointy-haired space witch trapped in an intergalactic dumpster for ten thousand years.

What was the first-ever costume you made?

My very first costume was Edward Scissorhands from the Tim Burton film [of the same name]. Made from garbage bags, duct tape, and pizza box cardboard, the costume was just fun to be in. Like Edward, my formative years were centered in that melancholy fantasy genre of storytelling, with inspirations from Gustave Doré, Edgar Allan Poe, and of course Tim Burton films.

You go to a ton of conventions. How do you decide which ones to attend?

> Conventions for me are a great way to network and have fun with my friends. There are the annual tentpole conventions that my friends and I attend: Katsucon in Washington, DC, C2E2 in Chicago, and New York Comic Con. Conventions have made positive strides in making their spaces friendly for cosplayers to have dedicated areas for showing off their creations, taking photographs, and hosting panels. The "cosplay is not consent" movement has empowered cosplayers to feel safer in their costumes, with convention staff taking action against people inappropriately touching or harassing cosplayers. Cosplayers want to have a good time in their costumes in a safe environment, and conventions have made that possible.

What advice would you give to kids who want to try cosplay?

> Remember that it is *play*. We're all just people having fun in costumes. Don't compare yourselves to others, and be nice to people cosplaying the same character as you. We're in this to have fun!

■ ■ ■ ■

As you gather your materials and get to crafting your next amazing cosplay, you might come across some words, phrases, or other things that you don't know. Good news, we have a handy glossary on page 125 that will help you navigate this cool new space.

CHAPTER THREE

Hey, Listen

COMPARED TO OTHER EXPRESSIONS OF fandom in this book, podcasting is but a baby. Picture podcasting like the Child, affectionately known as Baby Yoda, from *The Mandalorian*, toddling its way through the world. All kidding aside, the realm of modern podcasting has grown exponentially since its beginning in the early 2000s. A podcast is a digital audio file, usually available as an episodic series, that can be downloaded by listeners. Podcasters record the audio file, and listeners, or subscribers, to the podcast receive new installments through their computers or mobile devices. Think of it like radio, but online.

In truth, audio releases in this style stretch back through the decades; it was once called *audio blogging*, which is basically the old-timey word for podcasting. Without internet access and digital playback devices, audio blogging didn't come close to having the widespread reach and popularity then that podcasts have today. And, let's be honest, "audio blogging" doesn't sound as catchy as podcasting, does it?

HISTORY LESSON: THE TERM *PODCASTING*

The term *podcasting* replaced *audio blogging* in the early 2000s. You can trace the etymology, or origin, of the term *podcast* to 2004. Journalist Ben Hammersley created the word in an article for the British newspaper *The Guardian*; he combined the terms *iPod* and *broadcast* to make *podcast*. Pulling *broadcast* from the radio world and *iPod* from Apple's revolutionary (for the time) portable media player, Hammersley inadvertently coined a word that would be used for the burgeoning medium. Back then, podcasting was considered an experiment that could succeed or fail. It leveled the playing field, allowing anyone with a recording device and the time to become a broadcaster—they could talk about politics, news, their fandoms, anything.

You most likely listened to a podcast today or have a favorite one, so you probably know podcasting took off and was successful. However, as more enthusiasts pressed the Record button, distribution technology leaped to catch up. Liberated Syndication, or Libsyn, launched as the first-ever podcast service provider in 2004, and then Apple's iTunes built in everything users needed to discover and listen to podcasts in 2005. Today, there are numerous ways for podcasters to deliver their episodes to subscribers. The addition of social media amplifies a podcaster's signal, too, allowing them to reach even more potential listeners around the globe in more ways than ever before. Now, anyone with an idea for a podcast, maybe one all about *Star Wars* or *Lord of the Rings*, can create and launch one.

In 2006, the first podcast award shows kicked off, and some companies offered podcasters payment to produce content for them. Popular shows started getting hundreds of thousands of downloads each month, which meant that shows like *Serial* or *Radiolab* became household names and helped increase the popularity of the medium. Each year, more and more people listen to at least one show on a regular basis, and it's easier than ever to find a podcast (or two) about any topic.

Of course, that means that you, too, can make a podcast. Podcasts are the perfect outlet for enthusiastic, thoughtful gushing about any fandom, character, or topic that you feel passionate about. Take a moment to think about all the things you love, and see if you can narrow your mental list to one or two things that you want to talk about and discuss so badly that you can barely contain yourself. Chances are that's the best topic for you to start a podcast on. Also, with all the different distribution methods available, you can start recording and release your podcast for a small cost or maybe even for free.

STUFF YOU MISSED IN HISTORY CLASS

Holly Frey and Tracy V. Wilson host
the *Stuff You Missed in History Class* podcast.

What was your first fandom?

Tracy: *Pac-Man.* I was six. Of course, the idea of "fandom" would have been totally different in the early 1980s, and my participation in it as a six-year-old didn't really compare to later fandoms. But we were an Atari family, and we had *Pac-Man* and its successors to play at home. I had *Pac-Man* T-shirts and a *Pac-Man* board game, and I loved the Hanna-Barbera Saturday morning *Pac-Man* cartoon.

Holly: *Star Wars*! Seeing it for the first time, I fell in *love* with all the aliens and the fact that it was a galaxy populated by all kinds of different beings and none of them were considered weird. There wasn't really much fandom back then—it was kinda just me and two of my friends playing in the backyard. It wasn't until I was an adult that I really found fandom the way we think of it today; it was such a marvel that other people loved the same thing as I did! It felt like found family. We all lived very different lives and came from different backgrounds but somehow all spoke the same language.

What's the most challenging thing about releasing a podcast frequently and consistently?

> Holly: Our show is heavily researched with a lot of writing and prep before we ever sit in front of a mic. So it can get a little exhausting to always have a deadline looming.

What advice would give to kids who want to start podcasting?

> Tracy: You can start one right now if you're interested. You probably have all the technology you need in your pocket. But make sure that you're very ready to commit to publishing on a regular schedule and stick with it.

Getting Started

Before you get too wrapped up in choosing a podcast style or format, you should put some—actually, a lot of—thought into your topic. What will be the core subject matter of your podcast? You can be broad, or you can be more specific in your approach. You could make a general interest the connective tissue—like video games, comics, or fierce female heroines. One idea is to make a fandom-specific podcast, like the *Harry Potter* podcast *MuggleCast*. It's up to you how specific you want to be and what you want to talk about; just remember it should be a topic you're passionate about and interested in talking about. Take some time to consider how much you think you can discuss whatever your topic is, too. Get a blank sheet of paper and write your proposed topic in the middle and circle it. Around that circle, write down specific show ideas based on that topic. Circle those ideas and connect it to your topic with lines. If you end up with several lines and ideas on your paper, that's a good indication that you'll have plenty to say about it.

Once you've chosen a topic, it will help you find the best podcast format and tone. Do you want to be informative and serious? Or is being lighthearted more your speed? Tone will evolve as you become more comfortable recording, so sink into whatever is easiest, but try to keep it consistent from episode to episode. Once you have a topic, take a moment to cheer. Then you can get ready to record. You only have to figure out a few more pieces before you open your recording software of choice and press that red button.

First of all, come up with a name. The name of your podcast should in some way nod to the topic you've chosen, whether it's directly or through a pun. Otherwise, go crazy and come up with lots of options to choose from. Enlist your family, friends, and cohost (if you have one) to help. This is another part to take your time with, because you don't want to have to change your name later.

Next, give some consideration to how long you want your episodes to be and how often you want to release them. If you're going to put out an episode every week, shorter episodes are preferred. Looking at a monthly release? Then record for sixty minutes. However, there are no hard-and-fast rules about podcast length. Once you come up with a release schedule, do your best to stick to it. It's better to start with a monthly release and increase to more frequent installments at a later date.

Then, think about structure for your episodes. Write an outline and build regular segments, if you want to include them, into the beginning or the end of the episode. For instance, say you chose video games for your topic. You could add a segment where the hosts talk about which games they're currently playing and what they like or dislike about them. Your outline, sometimes called *show notes*, is supremely valuable to prepare ahead of recording. You can fully script some aspects like the introduction and sign-off, however, for everything in between, it's a good idea to list some bullet points rather than have a detailed script. The notes will guide the conversation and ensure you discuss everything you want to. Work on these with everyone making your podcast in a shared document to make things easier.

Filler words are all the things we say when we're trying to formulate our next sentence, such as *like*, *you know*, and *um*. With practice, you can cut down on your usage of these words when you speak. Removing filler words will ensure your message is clear, plus you'll sound more polished. Once you learn your way around editing, you can remove filler words from the final audio file, too.

Finally, make sure that you practice ahead of time. Do a full test episode or a brief segment and play it back so you can hear what you sound like. This is a good way to test your audio equipment and sound levels, and it will help you decide if you want to adopt a different tone or maybe sit closer to your microphone. When you feel more confident about the audio quality and the content, press Record for real. It's a huge milestone, and you should be so proud.

Podcast Formats

First and foremost, know that you have the freedom to create any kind of podcast you want. The styles below are only guidelines to help you get started; feel free to follow one of these to the letter, mix and match, or do a whole new thing. Listen to existing podcasts for format inspiration and ideas, but don't let those styles constrain you and your big ideas. Plus, keep in mind that some formats and styles work better than others depending on your chosen topic.

GOING SOLO

You don't have to create a podcast alone, but you certainly can. When going solo, you are the one pulling everything together from research and notes, to hosting, to producing. While that may sound like a lot of work, solo podcasts can be more straightforward because you only

have to go to one person for all the answers. However, doing a solo podcast doesn't mean you can't ask for assistance from others when you need it, whether it's for editing or for topic ideas. Don't be shy about asking others to spread the word about your show either. Use all the knowledge and resources you can gather to enable you to sit down and record with confidence.

One tricky aspect of recording a solo podcast is keeping in mind that you don't have someone else to bounce ideas off of or to offer a difference of opinion on the show. Try to keep a loose script or notes to help keep you on course, but try not to read verbatim from your notes unless you've practiced doing this until your reading sounds natural and conversational. Listeners will tune in for your personality and voice, so don't forget to have fun when recording, because when you're having fun, so are your listeners. Examples of excellent podcasts created and produced by one person include *Flash Forward* and *Lore*.

COHOSTING

On the other hand, cohosted, conversational-style podcasts are a total blast because it's like you're simply pressing Record while you chat with a buddy about something you both love or a topic that you're both eager to delve into. All you have to do is ask a friend to join you, either in person or through a call-recording service like Skype, as your cohost. You can have more than one cohost, too. One of the benefits of having cohosts is that all of you can brainstorm show topic ideas and notes, plus you can share the more technical responsibilities like editing and uploading the show.

Even though this type of podcast should be loose and fun, you'll still need to put some kind of organization in place so you don't go off the rails. Making loose outlines and putting one host in charge of gently steering the conversation back on track will help you remain focused and make it easier for your listeners to follow along. Don't forget to schedule extra time to socially catch up with your fellow hosts before or after you record an episode, too. That way you don't end up doing it during the show. Check out *Stuff You Missed in History Class* or *The Past and The Curious* for great examples of podcasts that have more than one host.

INTERVIEW

What if you want to do a podcast but don't want to be the center of attention? If you do want to create a podcast without being the primary voice and maybe don't have a cohost readily available, try making an interview podcast. You'll choose guests and ask them questions about different topics. It's better to have too many questions for your guests than not enough. Ask an older family member to help you reach out to potential guests that have opinions about or expertise in your show's topic, and ask them to come onto your show. For a more varied, and more challenging, interview format, you can also assemble a panel of guests to answer questions and discuss a certain topic. *The Show About Science* and *Tumble* are both great examples of this type of podcast.

It's also important to note that you don't have to be in front of the mic to get involved in podcasting. Just like with cosplay, there are plenty of support roles that you can take on behind the scenes by researching and developing content (researcher), helping make the podcast sound as great as it can (sound editor), keeping everyone on track (producer), or helping get the word out about your cool podcast (social media lead).

NONFICTION NARRATIVE

Do you like researching and writing essays or papers for school? Is your class notebook piled full of notes and facts? These types of writing and research skills are key to making a nonfiction storytelling podcast like *This American Life* or *Brains On!* To find a story—probably a headline from the news or maybe in the case of fandom, perhaps how a movie, game, or TV series was made—you'll need to dig in for a ton of research and come up with an engaging way to present it so it doesn't sound like you're reading a school paper. Making a nonfiction storytelling podcast is a challenge, but if you have an idea for it, believe in yourself, and get to outlining.

RADIO DRAMAS AND ROLE-PLAYING

To flip that idea a little, maybe you want to step outside of reality and introduce listeners to a world you create. That's where fiction storytelling podcasts shine, and if writing fiction makes your heart sing, then this the format for you. Fiction storytelling podcasts can have more of an audio drama style like *Welcome to Night Vale* or can be a recording of your role-playing session (check out page 71 to learn more about this type of gaming) like in *d20 Dames*. Whether you're writing a serialized story that will air over a few episodes or making stories as you go à la an RPG, you'll likely need to help of some friends. Do you know anyone who likes to perform different voices or act? They would be ideal for reading your work in your fiction storytelling podcast.

An RPG, or role-playing game, is a game in which the players assume roles of characters in a fictional world or story.

HYBRID

You can also mix and match any of these podcast styles and make a hybrid podcast. Work with a cohost to make an interview podcast. Pause your nonfiction narrative storytelling for a panel discussion or an out-of-story episode about the people who make the podcast. Stretch those creative muscles by being flexible and trying new combos. You'll want to have some consistency in your podcast as a whole, because listeners like knowing what to expect, but know you are allowed to get creative and that you don't have to commit to just one of these formats all the time—especially when you're trying to determine which podcast format you like the most. For example, if you're doing a solo podcast and occasionally want to conduct interviews or have guest hosts on, that's totally fine. Or perhaps you're having trouble scheduling time with your cohost(s) and you need to go solo for an episode. That is okay, too.

And remember you can apply any of these various formats to different podcast topics, such as science, mystery, comedy, fandom, your favorite video game, and more. It's about mixing and matching until you have the format that fits your show the best. Plus, you can experiment with one of these formats for a limited series podcast—a podcast with a set number of episodes—and try something else for your next podcast.

FANDOM MATH

PODCASTING + GAMING

Broadcast your passion for gaming with a podcast. No matter what kind of gaming you're into, you can talk about it by yourself or with friends. You can make a podcast to record your thoughts on newly released board games, to share tips and tricks about the video games you play, or to play a role-playing game.

— PODCAST SPOTLIGHT —

ROSE EVELETH

Rose Eveleth is the producer and host
for the *Flash Forward* podcast.

What was your first fandom?

I'm a fan of many things, but I'm not someone who feels like they're part of a fandom per se. To me, a fandom is a community of people who come together around some kind of media, and while I have friends who also like the things I like, I am not sure that I really have ever felt like I was truly a part of a broader community of people purely based on being fans of something.

What inspired you to start *Flash Forward*?

I started *Flash Forward* as a way to try to think about possible (and not so possible) futures and how we might get there. I think it can often feel impossible to change the future. Many of us feel helpless as we watch events unfold, and it can feel like there's nothing we can do to make tomorrow better. That's not true, and *Flash Forward* is all about finding the places we can change things and the people we can push on who can make things brighter. Launching the show was the easy part; the hard part has been keeping it going for over five years as a totally independent podcast. *Flash Forward* has no publication or wealthy benefactor keeping it going. It's funded instead by fans and patrons who give to the show to keep the futures coming, and I couldn't be more thankful to those folks.

How do you brainstorm show topics?

It's easy! Once you start thinking, *What if* . . . there are an endless number of possibilities. Try it now—look out the closest window and pick any object you can see. Then think, *What if we didn't have that?* There you go—that's a possible future. What if we didn't have cars, or birds, or trees, or telephone wires? That's a possible topic. I also read a lot of both research and science fiction to inform my ideas, and often I pull from books I'm reading or new research that's come out to create episodes. The fun part of the show is that you really can consider almost anything. Nothing is off-limits. The future hasn't happened yet!

What advice would give to kids who want to start podcasting— especially on the producing side of things?

My advice to anybody who wants to make a podcast is this: focus on the idea, not the tech. It's easy to get sucked down an endless tunnel of posts and internet arguments about which mic is better or which editing software is better. But none of that matters if your idea isn't solid, if you don't know why you're making the show you're making, and what you want the audience to get out of it. Before you touch any recording equipment, you should think about what it is that this show is about, why it matters now, who the ideal listener is, and what's going to keep the show fresh and exciting (for you, the creator, and for your listeners) for a long time to come. If you can't plan out ten episodes that make you excited, that's a red flag! Ideas are way more important than microphones.

READY PLAYER TWO

You've completed every step of launching a podcast so far, and all that is left is editing your show and sharing it with the world. You've done so much hard work already, so tap an older family member to lend you a hand and help guide you through what you'll need to do to produce your podcast and publish it online or to a podcast platform.

First things first, you and your helper need editing software. Fortunately, you can get free programs like Audacity or GarageBand to handle the basics. Video tutorials will assist you in learning how to use these tools and in giving you extra tips to make your podcast the best it can be. Next, you'll need to decide hosting for your podcast, which just means where you'll upload your podcast for it to be distributed into audio feeds of eager listeners. This is something you'll definitely need to get permission and guidance from your parent or guardian before doing. You can use free hosting platforms like Anchor, or you can upload directly to iTunes, Spotify, or Stitcher, which have different plan levels, user-friendly features, or special built-in systems. Take the time to research the different platforms available with your older family member or guardian to see what is best for you.

Ambient sound is any background noise present while you're recording. Your neighbor mowing their lawn is ambient sound. The plane flying overhead is ambient sound. Audio editors are responsible for removing undesired background noises.

Once your podcast is uploaded, you'll need to get the word out to your friends and family. Brainstorm with an older family member and decide if you want to build a simple, free website for your podcast, set up social media accounts, or maybe even create a zine to tell people about your new podcast. Interacting with your listeners is a great way to show others how awesome your podcast and the community around it are, and all these platforms are a great way to do just that.

MAKING-IT-HAPPEN TOOL KIT

Podcasting tools can range from very simple and free or low-cost to high-end microphones and sound boards with mixers. As with any of your fan creations and projects throughout this book, it's always great to start small and see what happens. You can always add more gear to your wish list as time goes on. Some key basics for your podcasting starter kit include:

Headphones with microphone • Smartphone with a recording app
• External microphone • Computer • Free recording software,
such as Audacity or GarageBand

All these components are available in different styles and at varying price points, but remember that the content of your podcast is more important than how you record it. You want to make sure listeners can clearly hear all your brilliant insights and conversations, but any other bells and whistles are optional. Seasoned podcasters will have different thoughts about equipment and what works best for them, so if you meet any podcasters, go ahead and ask them what they recommend for a podcast novice.

HISTORY LESSON: INTERNATIONAL PODCAST DAY

Podcasters and their listeners celebrate International Podcast Day annually on September 30. The podcast powerhouse day actually began as a national day in the United States in 2014. But in 2015, the founders realized podcasts were an international phenomenon, so the event became International Podcast Day in 2015. Podcasters from fifty-five different countries have joined in the festivities in the years since then, live streaming hundreds of hours of podcasts and trending on social media platforms with #InternationalPodcastDay.

Steve Lee had the idea for the special holiday of sorts in 2013 after realizing that so many things have designated days—like National Ice Cream Day or National Cat Day. So why not devote a calendar date to podcasts? It's a day when the people behind International Podcast Day can highlight resources and tools for podcasters. In addition to live broadcasts around the world with hosts sharing their personal stories and podcast know-how, podcast creators and fans gather at social events and local meetups around the globe to honor this medium.

— PODCASTER SPOTLIGHT —

MARC BERNARDIN

Marc Bernardin writes for TV series including *Masters of the Universe: Revelation* and *Castle Rock*, and he hosts the *Fatman Beyond* and *Battlestar Galacticast* podcasts.

What was your first fandom?

Well, I'll tell you, my first fandom was *Star Wars*. I think it's because I was eight years old when I saw it in the theater. At that age, you're beginning to build the parameters of the world as you understand it—and *Star Wars* is a perfectly good way for a kid to understand the concepts of good and evil. I liked that Luke Skywalker was a kid from the middle of nowhere with nothing. Granted, I wasn't born on a farm—moisture or otherwise—but I grew up pretty poor. And the idea that greatness could come from anywhere was really powerful. Plus, the Millennium Falcon is super cool.

You write TV series, you host and cohost podcasts. Did you ever think it would be your career?

As for podcasting, I never thought this is something I'd be doing professionally. It ultimately took a friend of mine who had a podcast inviting me on his to get me into it. Over time, though, I think I started to get pretty good at it. That's the key to new things: you're going to stink at everything at first. But the more you do it, the better you'll get at it.

What advice would you give to a kid who wants to start a podcast?

If you want to start your own podcast, you absolutely should. And if you have a friend you can do it with, even better, because conversation with two people is much more interesting that a conversation with yourself. And if there's a topic you both love—but have different perspectives on—that's gold. Podcasts are, at their core, about either offering information or sharing love. Teaching or preaching. So don't start your podcast until you feel comfortable doing one or the other.

■ ■ ■ ■

As you press Record and get into the world of podcasting, you might come across some words, phrases, or other things you don't know. Check out our glossary on page 125 that will help you figure things out.

CHAPTER FOUR

Press Start

GATHERING AROUND A TABLE WITH friends and family to play a game is a tradition that reaches back through history and all walks of life—picture cowboys dealing out cards for poker on a grimy table in an old Western saloon or wealthy Regency-era lords and ladies gathering around a paisley-fabric-covered card table for a game of whist. Nowadays, the term *gaming* includes a much broader spectrum of games like tabletop games, role-playing games, and video games.

The growing interest in pop culture and expansion of types of games have helped gaming explode into something bigger and better than ever before. Gaming stands apart from some of the other communities in this book, because it can be both a way to express and expand your fandom as well as a fandom in and of itself. For example, you could be interested and enjoy playing games regardless of the subject or format, or you could be interested in games specifically tied to a fandom you enjoy, like LEGO or *Batman*. Whatever your interest, you'll have no trouble finding piles of games to try out.

You can choose the level at which you want to engage with games: sit down and play games as others have designed them, which is completely cool, or leave your own mark by creating something new, which is also cool. That can mean doing something like adapting a board game's rules to suit your needs and adjusting as you play to create a better experience for the group. Or maybe envisioning a world for a role-playing game and creating all the beings that populate it. Or if you're into programming, you can learn to design and code a video game. Yet another creative option is to build your own area in an existing video game like *Roblox*. Think about what feels right for you based on your interests and talents, and then get to work.

Game Types

Gaming isn't just about video games or board games. There are tons of options for different styles of gameplay in various settings. It can be overwhelming, so let's break down a few types of games you can start exploring and how you can put your own creative stamp on them. We'll also go into how you can get started with each of these types of games.

TABLETOP GAMES

Board games like *Monopoly* and *Ex Libris* in the cabinet, the deck of playing cards in the drawer, or your deck of *Magic: The Gathering* cards are all examples of tabletop games. The most basic definition for tabletop games is "games that are played on a table." Yep, that's it. Of course, the number of games one can spread on a flat surface and play is impossibly large and includes popular pastimes such as chess and mah-jongg to contemporary titles like *Ticket to Ride* and *Munchkin*. Now places like game cafés are popping up everywhere,

and it seems like new games are released every week. Seriously, look at the game section next time you go to the store. It's always growing.

Some different types of tabletop games include card games, dice games, board games, strategy games, cooperative games, puzzle games, and miniature-based games. Whew. These categories have games of every flavor from trivia to romance to science fiction. The wonderful thing about having so much variety is that you're almost guaranteed to find a style of game that you and your friends or family enjoy playing together. And if it's hard to get other players to sit down with you, there are plenty of single-player games to try out as well. Experiment to learn which style and genre of game you like the best. You can do this by asking your local game store or game café about events, since many shops have beginner sessions where you can learn and play with other beginners. Also keep an eye out for gaming conventions in your area, because that's a great opportunity to find gaming groups, demo new games, and dip your toes into the world of game development and design.

When it comes to creating your own tabletop games, you can choose to start from scratch or make modifications on an established game. If you have a vision for a new tabletop game you want to make from the ground up, then go for it. Write a rule book as you brainstorm and develop your game to keep track of everything. Use your crafting skills and household objects to help construct your vision. When you think it's ready, then it's time to playtest the snot out of it with your friends and family to see what works and what needs further tweaking. When you have the game working just as you like it, ask for assistance in making a more durable, final version to share with friends and pull out during parties and game night.

To playtest a game means to check for design flaws and make sure the rules make sense for the gameplay.

Another way to add a little more personality and difficulty to a tabletop game is to rework the existing game and its pieces. One way to do this is to modify the rules. For example, house rules are rules that only apply when you play the game with specific people or at a specific place. Another way to modify a game is through personalization. If you have a game with miniatures, then paint outside the lines and give them a unique style. Miniature painting is a blast of a hobby that will improve your attention to the tiniest of details. With card games like the *Pokémon Trading Card Game*, you can use your tastes to build a deck that only has the cards that you want—like a deck using only fairy-type Pokémon or a deck with Pokémon from a specific region.

ROLE-PLAYING GAMES

Does the idea of taking on a role in a fictional universe sound appealing to you? Then you might want to try a role-playing game, also known as an RPG. This type of game varies wildly with tabletop RPGs, RPG video games, and even live-action role-playing games like Larping. Regardless of which style of RPG you want to try, the idea is that you're playing a character, and you have control of the character's decisions and actions and are experiencing the story through their point of view. Whether your character is the sort who helps others in the game or wants to take over the fictional universe you're playing in, it is all up to you.

Dungeons & Dragons is an example of a popular, well-known tabletop RPG (TTRPG), but it is far from the only kind of tabletop RPG available. Games like *Bubblegumshoe, Mouse Guard, Dinosaur Princesses*, and more are great options to try, and there are so many others available and being created every day that you're sure to find something to pique your interest. The same goes for video games.

You can play as Sora in *Kingdom Hearts* and decide which abilities you want to strengthen in his character as you team up with Disney and *Final Fantasy* characters in some of your favorite Disney worlds. If you're into a quieter RPG video game, maybe you'll want to explore the universe and discover new alien creatures in *No Man's Sky*. Employees at your local games shop will be more than happy to give you recommendations based on your interests and preferred style of playing, so don't be afraid to ask them.

But if you can't find an RPG that offers exactly what you're looking for, that's when it's time to think about designing a game of your very own. Picture it: a whole world that you've created for your friends to play in. This is the perfect time to brainstorm with friends and explore all the different ideas you have for your new game, as well as the different ways you can share it with your friends and community. You can bring it to life with pen and paper for a tabletop RPG or start programming a video game. Encourage your friends who like cosplay to turn your idea into a Larp session or for a podcast to interview you about your game and how you created it. Throw any ideas you have into it. And while developing rules and mechanics from scratch might seem like a huge task, don't forget that you can look to other games as examples. As long as you're being respectful of the original games and are clear with your community and friends that you are borrowing from others, feel free to mix and match mechanics from games you like and adapt the structure of other games to help support your idea as you learn how to develop a game. Document all of this in a notebook you'll use specifically for all your RPG dreams, and feel free to add sketches or anything else that inspires you.

—— GAMING SPOTLIGHT ——

KAT KRUGER

Kat Kruger writes for the entertainment and gaming industries.
She's the dungeon master for the *d20 Dames* podcast.

When did you first start playing RPGs, and what about them resonated with you?

It was 2014, around the time when *Dungeons & Dragons 5E* was released that I learned to play. In fact, that's how I met my partner. He was a program specialist for *D&D* at the time, and we both were guests at Hal-Con, a sci-fi con. What spoke to me immediately about the game was the collaborative storytelling element. As a young-adult writer at the time and onetime theater geek, I was pretty much hooked from the start.

How did you start making your passion for gaming your career?

After taking on the role of dungeon master for a home game shortly after learning to play in 2014, I decided to teach creative writing through *D&D* at the MacPhee Centre for Creative Learning. It wasn't until I moved to the West Coast that I even considered making the career change from freelance writer to narrative designer. The funny thing is, I used to code text adventure games as a kid, but it never occurred to me that I could do it for a living. I started off small, writing a couple of convention-exclusive one-shots, and then made the leap by starting the *d20 Dames* podcast with Jen Vaughn. Since then, I've published content from the show, run live shows at many conventions across Canada and the USA, written for Adventurers League, and contributed to several anthologies. I'm also the story architect for Multiverse, which is an innovative online platform for TTRPGs.

Do you have a go-to character class or type when you play RPGs?

In digital RPGs, I've always liked playing rangers because I feel like they're a good mix of melee, ranged, and a bit of spellcasting mixed in together. For tabletop, I've been experimenting with different classes. One of my fave characters is the Countess, who I played on *Adventure They Wrote*. She's a cleric of the trickery domain, which means she's a bit mischievous.

What advice would you give to kids who want to find or start a gaming group?

It's important to play with people you trust and who have a similar sense of what you find fun. Whether you're in it for combat, role-play, exploration, or any combination of those pillars of play, it's important to establish that early. A session zero is essential to determine that. Talk to everyone involved about what's expected, and keep checking in on each other. Things change, and that's okay. Open communication is really key to having a successful gaming group.

VIDEO GAMES

Gaming extends off the table and into the world of the internet and consoles with video games. Any electronic game that involves interacting with a screen can be classified as a video game—think *Tetris*, *Sonic the Hedgehog*, *Minecraft*, *Overwatch*. How many video games can you list in your head? How many do you have on your shelf? Go ahead, I'll wait.

You can choose a game for a single player, while some titles are suited for meeting up with your friends and people around the globe to quest or build. Video games can bring together fans with multiplayer modes or through IRL video game conventions. Like tabletop games, video games contain a plethora of different genres like massively multiplayer online role-playing games (MMORPGs), RPGs, first-person shooters, sports games, platformers, fighting games, adventure games, simulators, turn-based strategy games, educational games, and more. Video games have evolved from being tied to the traditional console, too. Mobile games are available through phones, and then there are augmented and virtual reality games. All of this means more people than ever can play video games. Some of these games take over a hundred hours of play to get through, while others are made for enjoying in a single afternoon.

HISTORY LESSON: ESPORTS

Shorthand for electronic sports, esports has become a growing industry in recent years, with whole leagues forming around esports competitions. Think of it as professional sports but played with video games rather than person-to-person contact. Teams often compete against each other in the same location with spectators, just like a more traditional sports match. When we talk about esports, modern events come to mind: league teams battling it out in *Overwatch* or gamers going all out in *League of Legends*. Those are both popular titles with hundreds of thousands of fans cheering on competing players and their respective teams. So it might be a surprise to learn that esports started just about fifty years ago.

One of the earliest known esports events occurred in 1972 at Stanford University. Their Artificial Intelligence Laboratory planned the tournament, focused on the '60s game *Spacewar!* In the game, two players each controlled a spaceship and battled each other. Stanford and other colleges became the host to similar esports events because they had the technology necessary to facilitate the matches. Today, some colleges even offer scholarships to esports players, and players can win tens of thousands of dollars in competitions. The total esports prize money awarded each year across multiple leagues right now is in the millions. Millions! Back then at that first *Spacewar!* tournament? The prize was a subscription to *Rolling Stone* magazine.

Advances in multiple areas of technology, from equipment to graphics to stronger broadband internet connections becoming more widely available, have contributed to esports gaining traction and becoming what it is today.

You can make a little esports action of your own by setting up a video game tournament with your gaming community.

Not sure where to start with finding new video games to try? Ask your parents or older family members if they have any games they enjoyed playing, or ask for recommendations from friends. Ask an adult to help you if you want to download any new games to play on whatever kind of device you have. Your best bet to find out what kind of games you'll enjoy is to experiment and try all the different types of video games that sound appealing. Hopefully, you find more than one world that completely enthralls you. And when you do, search to see how many games exist within that world. If you become obsessed with *The Legend of Zelda*, for example, you'll have a ton of titles to play.

Putting your own spin on video games can be as simple or as challenging as you want. Starting with the latter, you could create a video game from scratch. You'll need to brainstorm, design, and code the game. It will absolutely take some elbow grease, but it's not impossible—especially with the help of your parents, teachers, books, YouTube videos, and internet how-to guides. Alternatively, you can build your own world within another game. Sandbox video games like *Minecraft* or *Dreams* are a fantastic examples of this. These open-ended games have incredible customization controls that allow you—and your friends, if you want—to create buildings, spaceships, or entire cities in addition to characters and worlds. Your plans can be as elaborate or simple as you want with your ideas and games that you make.

We've covered several types of video games, but we haven't gone over everything. It would be almost impossible to capture all aspects of gaming, but hopefully this chapter shows you that gaming is not defined by any single title or particular type of game. You can truly find one or several little corners of gaming to call home in the vast space.

Avatar, not to be confused with the animated series or the James Cameron film, is a visual representation of the player in a video game or virtual world. This graphic of a user's online self can be two- or three-dimensional.

READY PLAYER TWO

Whether you want to read a thorough video game walk-through guide or watch a video with tips about how to be the most prepared, coolest game master ever, the internet is a great resource. You can learn more about one of your favorite games to your heart's content or research different games' inspiration to help make your own world. And hey, playing games together or just sharing your thoughts is one of the easiest ways to connect with friends and the community.

As you wade into your gaming fandom, talk with an older family member about what you'd like to dig through online or which games you want to play. You might find out that they are excited to play or share their experiences of the game with you. Even if they're not gamers, it is important to have them assist you in finding what you're looking for safely.

Remember, you don't have to go online to connect with others, and it is just as much fun to start gaming with your family and friends. All the types of games we discussed have options to fit your group no matter its size. Two players? Ten players? No problem. Your local gaming and hobby store or a game café are also fantastic places to learn more about different games and as a way to meet others within this community. Even your local library or comic book shop could be a great resource when looking for ways to connect and learn.

Crunchy is a reference to a style of gameplay that requires significant planning and strategy. Derived from the phrase *crunching numbers,* crunchy applies to any game requiring extreme mental application.

■ ■ ■ ■

FANDOM MATH
GAMING + COMMUNITY

One of the easiest ways—though definitely not the only one—to connect with a community is through gaming. Both tabletop and video games can, and often do, include multiple players, so the infrastructure is already there to help you meet and connect with new friends. Ask for assistance in finding a gaming or hobby store in your area and then check out their game schedules. Many shops have a running calendar packed with events featuring miniature games, deck-building hangs, and much more. No shop nearby? Recruit friends to play and try out different games and form your own gaming community.

— **GAMING SPOTLIGHT** —

ANNA PROSSER

Anna Prosser is an esports professional,
gamer, producer, and host.

What video games made you fall in love with gaming?

When I was very young, it wasn't as common for everyone to have a home computer, but my dad loved them and built us one. I played lots of DOS games on there, but *Commander Keen*, *Captain Comic*, and *Archon* were probably my favorites.

My grandma also had an Intellivision console, one of the earliest game consoles to be released! She kept it in mint condition and would bring it out to play with me whenever I came to visit. Our favorite games to play together were *Lock 'n' Chase* and *Night Stalker*. She still has it, but it takes a lot of adapters to make it work on a modern TV.

When did you know you wanted to make gaming part of your career, and what was that journey like?

Since gaming was a great way for me to connect with people I loved when I was younger, as I grew, I loved finding and becoming part of the communities around games. Coming together at the early stages of professional esports, the *StarCraft* community was the one that really pulled me in and made me think that I could make a career in gaming.

I fell in love with the *StarCraft* community because it was a group of people who were brought together over their love of a game but also liked to support each other and work together. I found that they not only loved real-time strategy gaming, but they loved to use strategy to solve real-world problems, too. Once, they helped me raise money for a charity so fast that we accidentally crashed the charity website. That kind of power and goodwill is what made me want to stay a part of the gaming community.

I knew I didn't want to be a pro gamer—I didn't have the time or the skill or the patience to become that good at any one game—but I did have education in speech communication and experience in front of the camera, so I set about trying to help tell the exciting stories of the gaming community through making video content. In that way, I found my place in the gaming community and eventually became respected for that work enough to make it my job. It was hard work, and it took a long time to build, but now I'm so thankful that my career was born out of genuine love for a powerful community.

What advice would you give to kids who want to get more involved with gaming and pursue it as a profession?

If you want to have a career in gaming (or, really, in any growing field), start by knowing yourself very well. Ask yourself questions like: What are you good at? What could you do over and over and still never get tired of it? What are the ways that you help other people best? Next, look at the industry or community that you want to be a part of, and think about where you can bring value. Ask questions like: What can I do well that companies need, or that not many other people are doing yet? How can I improve my skills in order to be an attractive person to hire or work with? Finally, reach out to the people that you want to work with, express your value, and either ask them how you can get involved or how you can be sure to get the education, experience, and skills that will make them want to work with you.

And try to keep your eye on what you love about gaming. That's what will give your career real longevity and make it feel fun.

■ ■ ■ ■

As you press A, roll dice, and explore the vast world of gaming, you might come across some words, phrases, or other things that you don't know. Don't worry! We have a helpful glossary on page 125 that will help you learn more about gaming.

CHAPTER FIVE

So Say We All

ONE OF THE BEST PARTS of fandom is being part of a community of like-minded people. These are people who get you and your passions. They like the same movies, games, books, or combination of things as you, so you'll always have plenty to talk about. Even though you have a lot in common, it is always good to remember that your points of view and opinions are yours, and others will have their own thoughts as well. When you join or start a community, ask the members lots of questions and be open to learning what others like and enjoy about the thing you love. They're bound to have different perspectives because of their unique life experiences, and these new perspectives from others often enrich your fandoms and help you enjoy them in new ways.

Learning about new ideas, perspectives, and ways to enjoy fandom are only a few of the many positive benefits of being part of a community. It's also a huge deal to have a space where you're comfortable being your most authentic self. You'll know a community is right for you when you feel comfortable and excited to turn to it when you positively, absolutely need to gush over Spider-Man's new costume or what happened on the latest episode of *Doctor Who*. If your community is the only place you feel like putting your enthusiasm and passion on display, then that makes your relationship with those friends all the more valuable. Don't be afraid to ask yourself if you think you can be your most fannish, wonderful self when you're with the other community members. If your answer is *yes*, then you've found your place. If the group isn't quite jibing for you, maybe give it a little longer and then start thinking about making your own space where you and others can share and enjoy things together.

**Fannish means of or relating to fans and fandom.
Going to a convention is fannish, and so is wearing cosplay.
If it's a fan activity, you can use this adjective to describe it.**

Being part of a community also means access to more resources, ideas, and support. Often, communities are more than willing to help you out, give advice, and listen to your ideas. If you're in a cosplay community or there are people interested in trying it out, you can lend extra materials or give advice to another cosplayer, or if you are the person who is trying to learn, feel free to ask other members for help and advice. If your community meets in person, perhaps you can have a lending library comprised of titles each of you contributes or you can make a list of all the podcasting gear or art supplies each of you own. Put whatever you (and older family members) are okay with sharing on the table. Split talents, too. For example, start a podcast within your community and find hosts, someone to design a logo, special guests, a tech expert—use teamwork to find roles for everyone.

FANDOM MATH
COMMUNITY + FANFIC

Sharing your fanfic with readers is almost as satisfying as writing it. You can keep your fanfic private if you want, but if you want to put it out in the world, you can start with a small community you know. Gather your friends, virtually or in person, for an afternoon of writing fanfic, encouraging one another (seriously, it's so reassuring to be in the writing trenches alongside others) and sharing what you've written. It's a tremendous way to get feedback and thoughts from pals that you trust. You could also do this within an online community in which you control specifically who can read your work.

Kinds of Communities

There are all kinds of communities and groups that you can join, including ones that meet in person or ones that meet virtually through websites or even video meetups. They can be big or small, local, national, or even global. Just remember that a community should be whatever makes you feel most at home and safe. If you find it easier to connect with others online through chat rather than a local meetup, that is totally fine—stick with what works for you. Of course, communities are fluid and change depending on the group, fandom, and when it was created, but here are a few examples of the main types of communities you might find out in the world of fandom.

FAN CLUBS

When thinking about how fans have connected over the last several decades, fan clubs are one of the first things that come to mind. These communities vary in group size, but they are easy to spot because they usually focus on and celebrate a specific thing or group in pop culture or a single celebrity. It is important to note that some companies create official fan clubs for the franchises they hold rights to, like the Official Harry Potter Fan Club, but most of the time, fans start and run them, like the Naruto Fan Club. Different groups of fans often create different clubs, so it is very likely that a single fandom may have a lot of fan club options, including "official" and regular fan clubs. After getting permission from an older family member, check online and see what fan clubs turn up for your different fandoms. If there's not an active club to join, then this might be the perfect time to start one yourself.

IN PERSON

Communities can be as small—just yourself and a handful of friends—or as large as you want. In-person fan communities gather everyone in the same physical space, making it a more natural place to take time to get to know one another. Face-to-face conversations always bring an element of closeness that can be harder with video calls or texts. Maybe your in-person community is about making fanart and will meet regularly and work on a project together or just cheer each other on while you're each working on your own projects. In that case, too, maybe your group will invite a professional artist or art teacher to come to one of your meetups to speak and give advice. The community could be focused on gaming, comic books (think about how many issues you could lend and borrow!), BTS, or *Gravity Falls*. If you are starting your own in-person community, then go as specific or as broad as you want, and if you are already part of one, then talk to members about how you can explore and expand your fandom together.

VIRTUAL

Virtual communities enable you to share and enjoy a fandom with others from around the world. Being part of this type of community means that you can learn, experience, and be inspired in ways that you might not have imagined, because dozens or hundreds of fans are able to express themselves within the group.

Of course, the ways in which online communities interact changes depending on available technology, so an app or a social media channel that is popular today may not be around tomorrow. For example, ask an older family member about Myspace. Current, popular virtual spaces for communities include Discord, a text, voice, and video chat app; forums for specific fandoms; Facebook groups; Reddit; and Tumblr. Whatever tool you use, be sure to ask an older family member to help check privacy settings to keep yourself and your data safe. And who knows, after you've safely connected with your virtual communities, maybe you'll have the opportunity to meet members in person one day at a convention or fan event.

HISTORY LESSON: CLUB JADE

Communities form around all aspects of fandom. In the case of Club Jade, a group of mostly female *Star Wars* fans formed an online *Star Wars* community in 1995. Named after Mara Jade, a popular character in a *Star Wars* series from the early '90s, Club Jade began as a mailing list. The members made this community around a single fictional character who has never appeared in a *Star Wars* movie. They started with discussions about Mara Jade and the novels by Timothy Zahn in which she appeared, so it was kind of like a fan club, but they grew into more than Mara Jade's cheerleading squad as they started branching out to bond together over the *Star Wars* saga as a whole. They even started a blog (clubjade.net).

Friendships that began in the Club Jade community's early days online have translated to real-life ones. Club Jaders still meet up in person regularly, whether it's at *Star Wars* Celebration or other conventions. A character in their fandom brought them together, and by creating this community online, they made the world smaller and more comfortable.

Getting Started

First things first, you'll need a name for your new group or community. Choose something straightforward like *Fandom* or *Character Name Fan Club*. Or get silly with it and throw in a pun or go "in world." Coming up with a name can be daunting, but a good way to get started is with a blank sheet of paper where you can write down everything that comes to mind. It doesn't matter if it's a complete name. Write down single words, sketches, phrases—seriously, whatever pops into your head. After doing this exercise for fifteen minutes, take a break, and then come back and see if you can play around with what you listed. If nothing satisfactory pops up, repeat the exercise. You'll come up with something fabulous in no time.

With your brilliant community name in hand, next you'll want to write a vision or mission statement. This should explain what you hope the community does for its members and your goals or reasons for making the community. For example, "I created Park Hoppers to bring together fans of *Kingdom Keepers* to discuss each book in the series and hopefully turn those discussions into podcasts." Your vision statement doesn't need to be lofty and can be something as simple as, "I made this community so we could all hang out and gush about who we're shipping." If you are starting the community with friends, it might be a good idea to share your vision statement with them first and ask if they have any ideas or suggestions before making it official. Then once everything is just the way you want it, go ahead and post it somewhere where all your members, both new and established, can see it.

Now it's time to find some members, which is a critical step in growing your community. First, look to the people you know. Do you have any friends or friends of friends that also love the same fandom as you? This is a terrific place to start, because you will already feel comfortable with the people you are inviting, and then that friend might have someone else in mind and can invite them, and so on. And just like that, your community has grown.

While meeting new people and growing your community is an important step, it is important to make sure that you figure out some other key factors before you start inviting tons of new members. After creating your community on paper, next you have to think about how your members will connect and interact with each other, which means figuring out a meeting space. If you'll be hosting in-person meetings and events, then scheduling, location, and space are all things you'll need to consider. If you are starting a virtual community, then you'll want to think about the best platforms to host your meetings and help members connect with each other. With both types of meetings, it is important that you and an older family member know and are comfortable with all the people in your group and that everyone knows that your community is a safe space. To help do this, you should get an idea of your initial community's group dynamics before you start adding other people. You want to make sure everyone gets along and feels comfortable around each other.

It's possible that no one in your friend group wants to have lengthy conversations about *Critical Role*, and maybe that's why you want to join or to start a community. With the help of older family members, you can start looking around where you live for a community to join. Check the local library and see if they have any groups that meet or if they have a community bulletin board where you could post a flyer. The same applies to your school and gaming, hobby, comic book, or bookstores. You can find community members by recruiting in places they already frequent. To give your efforts a little boost, wear any fandom gear you have while you're out and about. It's not 100 percent necessary, but you may run into other fans by letting your fan flag fly.

Once some members have joined and you've officially started your community, feel free to take it slowly and just watch, play, or read things in your fandom or just gather to chat. If you're itching to create, talk to your members about combining the talents of the community to plan a cosplay, make a fanzine, or start a podcast. Express yourselves and bond at the same time. Remember that you're all stronger together.

JORDAN DENÉ ELLIS

Jordan Dené Ellis runs geeky clothing company Jordandené and co-edits *The Sartorial Geek* with Liz Crowder Serota.

What was your first fandom?

My first fandom was *Pokémon*. I was pretty young, and I think it was one of the first times I tapped into pop culture. I loved how it was an instant connection with other kids: we could trade cards or link up our Game Boys, even if we didn't know each other super well. It was an instant ice breaker.

What inspired you to start Jordandené?

Jordandené started as a way to create the things I wanted to see in the world. At the time, well-designed, feminine, and geeky clothing didn't really exist. I wanted those things in my closet, and I suspected there might be other people out there who did, too.

Have you connected with other fans through your business?

Connecting with fans is actually my favorite part of running this business. I've been able to connect with fans in person at comic cons all over the country, both through having an exhibitor booth and by doing panels about geeky community and nerdy fashion. I've connected with customers online, mostly through Jordandené's ambassador program and by people sharing photos of themselves enjoying our products. These connections are so important to me that I started a second company, *The Sartorial Geek*, whose sole focus is creating a welcoming community for fans!

What advice would you give to kids looking to join or build a community centered on fandom?

If it doesn't already exist, make it! Now that we have the internet, there is a very good chance you can connect with someone else out there who enjoys the same things as you. If you can't find the kind of hang out you're looking for, you can start it. Chances are, other fans will really appreciate it.

■ ■ ■ ■

Keep in mind some important dos and don'ts when you're putting down the building blocks for your community.

- Do be welcoming to people and their feedback and contributions.
- Do be open-minded and curious.
- Do be respectful of everyone.
- Do be kind and positive.
- Do be encouraging.
- Do be enthusiastic and generous.
- Don't be a gatekeeper.
- Don't be a dictator.
- Don't be rude when you don't understand something.
- Don't have unfair expectations of community members.

Share these dos and don'ts with all your community's members so that you're all on the same page about making an awesome, uplifting place where you can all celebrate your fandom. Positivity should reign. Whatever else your community is, it should strive to be a safe and supportive place. You're all fans coming together to share your love for a fictional world; focus on that and you'll be golden.

Gatekeeping is a disrespectful circumstance that sometimes happens in fandom. This is when a person or a group limits access to a fandom usually based on subjective rules. For instance, someone saying you have to have played every *Super Mario* game ever to be a "real" fan of Mario, this is considered gatekeeping. You never have to prove yourself in any way to be a fan, though. If you like something, you're a fan. Welcome others who are just starting in the fandom.

READY PLAYER TWO

"It's dangerous to go alone! Take this," is a quote from *The Legend of Zelda* and is a good reminder to use caution when interacting with new people in person or online, especially if you are in a new or crowded environment like a convention. You most likely have already talked about general safety measures and have guidelines or rules set with your family, but don't forget to lean on your older family members for advice and help as you search for or start creating a fandom community. Not only can they help keep an eye out for red flags and make sure you stay safe, they also can help you set up things like a website with chat capabilities or a meeting time and place.

You can also team up with older family members to figure out designs and features you want to include on your websites or forums, plus they can assist with setting up special invitation links or pass codes for you to share only with your community members. It's all about working together. Be sure to share with them why this is important to you and what advantages you see in joining or starting a community. And never, ever hesitate to ask them for help if you run into issues with the community itself or difficulties with any community members.

COMMUNITY SPOTLIGHT

LIZ CROWDER SEROTA

Liz Crowder Serota is the cofounder and coeditor of *The Sartorial Geek*.

What was your first fandom?

My first fandom was probably *The Hobbit*. My grandma gave me an old dog-eared copy of the book when I was in the second grade, and I fell in love with it and the fantasy genre as a whole. I was a quiet kid who didn't love surprises or the unexpected, so seeing an anti-adventure main character like Bilbo Baggins face his fears and go on the adventure of a lifetime really resonated with me. It made me feel like introverts could be heroes, too.

What made you want to start *The Sartorial Geek*?

Our inspiration for starting *The Sartorial Geek* was the realization that living your best geeky life is about more than buying limited-edition merchandise or going to a new Marvel movie opening night. It's about that swell of something akin to joy when you realize that someone else in this vast universe plays the same obscure video game as you do. Or having an intense Twitter chat with a person you've never met in real life about shared *Game of Thrones* theories. Or an unspoken connection with the woman walking down the street repping your favorite Doctor on her shirt. We wanted to create a space that helped like-minded geeks find their people, at long last.

We also wanted to make geeky fashion more accessible to all body types, skin colors, genders, and even fandom levels. Our tagline is, "A community for the geek in all of us." And we truly mean that.

What community-building advice would you offer to kids?

Be kind. Be generous. Don't gatekeep (fandom is for everyone). If there's something you want to see in the world and it doesn't already exist, create it yourself! Also, even if you only find one other person in the whole wide world who likes the exact same thing as you, that's still a community, that's still valuable, and that still counts.

■ ■ ■ ■

As you build communities and interact with their members, you might encounter some words, phrases, or other things you don't know. Fortunately, you can flip to our handy glossary on page 125 for some guidance.

CHAPTER SIX

Going on an Adventure

BUILDING COMMUNITIES IS A WONDERFUL way to connect with other people in your fandom, but attending a convention is a way to take it to the next level. If you haven't been to a convention before, a good way to describe them is a place where large groups of fans can gather and celebrate their fandoms. Conventions can be broad and seemingly all-encompassing or niche and very specific, plus they can celebrate just about anything from cars to comics, video games, and even gardening. The big conventions you've most likely heard of are pop culture conventions and include a variety of fandoms and storytelling mediums.

But don't worry if you are looking for a convention that suits your tastes, because there are plenty to choose from. Like anime? Several anime conventions happen around the world, like Anime Expo or Sakura-Con, and they celebrate a wide number of manga and anime creators, shows, books, and more. You can even opt for an anime convention with a narrower focus like the Toronto Sailor Moon Celebration, a two-day convention centered on everything to do with *Sailor Moon*.

If you're a fan of something, then a convention focused on that thing you love probably exists, and you can join hundreds or maybe tens of thousands of folks who are passionate about the very same things as you. Pretty incredible, right? If an event with over one hundred thousand people isn't for you, don't stress, because conventions come in different sizes, too, so you can always find an event that is more in your comfort zone.

Lots of conventions have the word *comic* in their name, but that doesn't mean they're all about comic books. Conventions as we know them now largely got their start as small comic book conventions back in the 1960s—even though the first science fiction conventions took place before then. Early comic conventions focused on bringing comic book fans and creators together in a celebration of comics, especially because comics were in the midst of their Silver Age and flying off comic store shelves. Today, conventions are still helping people come together to celebrate things they love, and the *comic* part has stayed in names as a kind of nod and link to their origins, but now they include a bigger range of fandoms along with comics.

—— CONVENTION SPOTLIGHT ——
GALLIFREY ONE

And now for an example of a fandom specific convention: Whovians from around the globe travel to Gallifrey One in Los Angeles, California, to celebrate all things related to *Doctor Who*. Fans created the nonprofit event in 1989 and have run the convention annually since then. They've hosted nearly four hundred guests (!) specifically from the world of *Doctor*

Who and its spin-offs, including everyone from cast members to those behind the scenes. It's the world's largest and longest-running annual *Doctor Who* fan convention. You will never see as many TARDISes and TARDIS-inspired outfits at any other con or any other event, period.

READY PLAYER TWO

Conventions sound awesome, right? They are, and you're probably already itching to get to a con, don a lanyard, and have an amazing time as soon as possible. The good news is, because of the booming convention scene in recent years, you're all but guaranteed to find a con happening near you. Ask an older family member to help you find upcoming conventions that are happening nearby that you could possibility attend. Since new conventions get added to the calendar on a regular basis, it's hard to have an exhaustive list with all the conventions happening everywhere, so the best ways to find out about cons is to either ask your fandom community for insights or simply do an online search for your town's name and "conventions nearby." If nothing turns up, consider reaching out to local comics or game shops to see what they can recommend.

Getting Started

Once you've pinpointed a con that you cannot wait to go to, it's time to start thinking logistics. A convention's website or social media channels will have all the information you need to help plan your trip. You'll want to find out where the convention is located and talk with your family about getting there and whether the distance means you'll need to stay overnight. Next, you'll want to look at tickets and prices, and don't forget to write down the dates when tickets go on sale—you don't want to risk them selling out before you buy yours. Tip: The per-day cost often goes down the more days you go to the convention. Also, if you're dying to buy merchandise, meet celebrities, and get pictures or autographs while you are there, don't forget to plan for those costs, too; the sooner you can start saving, the better.

—— CONVENTION SPOTLIGHT ——

SAN DIEGO COMIC-CON INTERNATIONAL

If you've heard about any fan convention, it's probably San Diego Comic-Con International. Over 130,000 people attend the five-day con every summer in San Diego, California. Not only do fans attend by the thousands, the convention draws several Hollywood studios and actors in addition to a large stable of comic book publishers and creators. Whatever you're a fan of, it's likely represented somewhere—the exhibit hall, panels, cosplay—at San Diego Comic-Con. The convention's so big, it's spilled outside the San Diego Convention Center into the downtown San Diego area with local hotels and outdoor parks hosting additional panels and media events. But it wasn't always so massive.

San Diego Comic-Con had humble beginnings when it started in 1970. Then, it was called the Golden State Comic Book Convention. Taking place over three days at a hotel, three hundred attendees went to the event largely focused on comic books and the people who made them. The convention's name evolved until it became San Diego Comic-Con, now commonly referred to as SDCC, in 1973. Over the next twenty years, the convention grew, moving from a hotel to a smaller performing arts center. The con expanded on its focus from comics to broader pop culture. It's been at the San Diego Convention Center since 1991 and has grown every year with over one thousand panels programmed. The event's extreme popularity has made it notoriously challenging for people who want to attend to get tickets and a hotel room in the area. San Diego Comic-Con completely sells out year after year, but it is possible to go, and if you have the opportunity to see it firsthand, you should.

Planning Your Convention

Once you've chosen a con to check out, you have the enviable task of daydreaming about everything you'll see and do. Others in your fandom communities might have gone to that specific one or other conventions before, so ask them about their absolute favorite moments and what you cannot miss. Though each convention has its own voice and specialties, they all have a handful of components in common. The main thing to remember is that you'll have tons of things that you'll want to see and do. Try to make a list of the stuff that you *absolutely* have to see or do to help you remember, and keep track of your time while you are on the convention floor. It's almost impossible to get bored at a convention, but it is very easy to lose track of time or get distracted! Case in point, check out some of the many things you can do.

PANELS

Nearly all conventions offer programming that includes panels. Comic book creators, TV directors and writers, film stars, other fans, and everyone in between appear on panels. These discussions usually have a host or moderator who asks the panelists questions about the topic of the panel—for example: cosplay, *Supernatural*, time travel, or Marvel Comics. At bigger conventions, movie studios use these panels to debut new trailers or exclusive footage. Whatever the size of the convention, panels are a fabulous way to learn more about your fandoms and to see the creators and celebrities you like. Sometimes, audience members get a chance to ask questions, so you might be able to participate in the panel, too.

SHOPPING AND BROWSING

If you're more into the idea of browsing and maybe shopping, the exhibit hall area is for you. Vendors big and small set up tables in the convention's exhibit hall to sell toys, apparel, comic books, and so much more. Sometimes the point of a booth is to promote an upcoming movie or game, and sometimes the booth is there for fans to interact with the companies and creators who worked on those books, movies, games, and more.

ARTIST ALLEY

Look at a pop culture convention's website or programming guide and see if they have an Artist Alley. This is a must-visit area at any convention. Here, professional and amateur artists set up tables to sell their creations—such as original comic book pages, officially licensed art, fanart, fandom-inspired plush toys or jewelry, paper crafts, and so much more. Artist alleys blossomed from early comic book conventions where artists would meet and network with each other in the aisles. And now the wide variety of merchandise on Artist Alley tables is one of the main reasons to check it out. You never know what you'll find. It's seriously the best area to shop for unique gifts (you can even save your pennies to commission a piece of art just for you), and you'll be supporting independent artists and writers.

But more importantly, Artist Alley areas allow you to meet your favorite creators and perhaps get some advice. Be respectful of a creator's time—especially if they have a crowd of con-goers looking at their wares or waiting in line to get something signed—but when they're free, go ahead and ask questions about their work or the fandoms present in their work. And don't feel bad about looking even if you don't have extra money to purchase anything; creators will appreciate you expressing enthusiasm about their art.

Sometimes video game publishers like Capcom or Square Enix will set up stations alongside their booths with screens and controllers for attendees to try out upcoming titles, while board or tabletop game publishers have stations with tabletop, boards, or card games and pieces. Exhibit halls are full of activity and excitement, but they are also a great place to window-shop if you don't want to spend money or if you're looking for inspiration. Tip: Companies sometimes hand out freebies like posters, pins, and even T-shirts, so keep your eyes open.

COLLECTIBLES

But maybe you've been reading a lot about collectibles and saving your funds. Because that's a massive part of conventions, too. Lots of toy and apparel companies will sell items for the first time at specific conventions or offer convention exclusives, which is merchandise available at that convention only. Some attendees go to certain conventions for the sole purpose of acquiring limited-edition collectibles for themselves or friends. If you're into collecting, look at the convention's website to see the list of exhibitors. If LEGO, for example, will be at the convention, then you can investigate whether they'll be offering any show exclusives. Then the next part is reading about any rules or steps that you'll need to take for acquiring that exclusive.

Some companies will have people start lining up hours before the exclusive will be available, while others have lotteries to level the playing field, and some may only have a small quantity in stock each day of the convention. It widely varies by company and convention, so you'll need to carefully plan how to acquire that fancy LEGO minifigure, limited-edition Funko, or special enamel pin available at the convention for only a single day.

Of course, you can collect more than merchandise, such as autographs. Conventions know you want autographs from comic creators and/or celebrities, so they plan for it. Many cons have photo ops available with celebrities, too. Pursuing signatures means a little more planning to check out hours, restrictions (they may only be allowed to sign certain comics or photos, for instance), and costs. Remember to be respectful of the time of the person signing.

COSPLAY

That cosplay you've been working diligently on? Bring it to the convention! Hundreds of cosplayers attend every convention, so you'll be right at home. Maybe you'll run into others wearing costumes from the same fandom, or even the same costume. Nerd out with them about how you crafted your costumes and the subjects of those cosplays. Then give yourself a pat on the back when you're done because you're expanding your fandom community with every interaction. As an extra bonus, several cons have cosplay competitions that you can participate in or that you can sit back and watch as an audience member. There are also conventions like Dragon Con that put a ton of emphasis on cosplay and include activities like a massive cosplay parade that goes through the streets of downtown Atlanta, Georgia.

FANDOM MATH
CONVENTIONS + COSPLAY

Conventions and cosplay are natural companions, like peanut butter and jelly. People have even started conventions specifically for cosplayers to gather, show off their costumes, and attend how-to workshops. It's an opportunity to pack and wear a new costume for each day of the convention, get high-quality pictures taken by skilled photographers, and go to panels featuring your favorite cosplayers.

As conventions expand and outgrow convention centers, you might have noticed that certain programs and events have started taking over the area near the convention center, too. That means you might find activations, events, panels, and more nearby, and some may not even require a convention badge. Activations are events that help immerse you in a replica set from a movie or TV series or set you in the middle of an obstacle course. For example, Warner Bros. did a whole *Detective Pikachu* walk-through with a ton of Instagrammable moments to help promote the movie. When you stop by an activation, you should always ask about prizes and giveaways as well.

Formed from the words *convention* and *ennui*, which means a feelings of sadness and dissatisfaction, connui is something you may feel when you leave a convention and come back to the real world.

Convention Pro Tips

The first step of going to a convention is accepting that you probably won't be able to do everything that you want to do. You'll see so many cool things on the convention website, but not enough hours exist in the day to do it all. In the end, it just comes down to the math, but you can maximize the hours you're at a convention with a little planning.

Conventions typically post their full schedule of activities at least two weeks before the event. First, think about what your priorities are for the convention. Maybe you want to focus on getting convention-exclusive collectibles, to see a panel featuring an actor from your favorite movie or TV series, to meet an author you admire, or to wander around and soak it all in. There is no wrong answer, so tailor your time to help you do exactly what you want to do.

With your top five priorities in mind, sit down with an older family member to look at the convention's schedule—scroll through each day to ensure that you don't miss anything. As you browse, take notes on a piece of paper or in a text document of any activities or events that interest you. That can be a panel happening at a specific day and time, or if it's something like RPG miniature painting, that's available every day during exhibit hall hours. Or it might even be a toy company doing a giveaway at their booth at a certain time.

Once you've gone through the whole schedule, take a look at your notes and choose up to three activities total, or choose one thing for each day of the convention that you don't want to miss out on, and write them down in a notebook that you'll take with you. It might be a good idea to list three additional items as backups. Now you'll know the times and places that the things most important to you are going on, and you can plan the rest of your convention time around those things, which guarantees you'll have a more positive convention going experience.

— CONVENTION SPOTLIGHT —

MCM LONDON COMIC CON

The Movie Comic Media (MCM) Expo Group organizes a number of pop culture conventions in the United Kingdom every year, with the biggest one taking place in London. The MCM London Comic Con usually

happens twice each year at ExCeL London; the convention lasts for three days. Founded in 2001 as the London Movies, Comics, and Media Expo, the event has many of the usual convention features, including special guests, an extensive exhibit area, and a comic village for creators and publishers to sell their comics. The convention is particularly known for cosplay with its MCM Fringe Festival, a festival within the con designed for cosplayers to make plans for meetups, photo shoots, and hangouts.

Convention Dos and Don'ts

Going to your first convention can be like visiting a strange new world. You might be nervous about going, but as long as you are polite and kind, you'll be just fine—promise. Along with your general manners, here are a few dos and don'ts to help you with some convention specific etiquette:

- Do be mindful of how much space your costume takes up. You don't want your wings to knock people in their faces all day.

- Do ask cosplayers if it's okay for you to take a picture before you do so. Cosplay does not equal consent.

- Do ask artists if you can take a photo of their merchandise.

- Do respect lines for giveaways or signings, and don't cut in front of anyone.

- Do ask an older family member to help you review any guidelines on the convention's website.

- Don't put your stuff (especially drinks and foods) on exhibitors' and artists' tables while you're shopping.
- Don't stop in the middle of a busy aisle or in front of an escalator. Get out of the way before you take a picture or text someone.

What to Pack

After you choose your outfits and neatly organize every piece and accessory you need for your cosplay, you're ready to figure out what you should carry for a day at a convention. The trick is balance; you'll want to have essentials to make your day more comfortable, but you don't want to weigh down your shoulders or have a bag so stuffed that it bumps into everyone while you're walking. Plus, you'll want to leave room for all the treasures you'll get! Here's where to start:

- Refillable water bottle
- Light snacks like granola bars, fruit snacks, or small protein bars
- Permanent marker just in case you want an autograph
- Pen
- Cash (only bring the amount you're allowed to spend)
- Travel-size hand sanitizer (and use it frequently)
- Camera
- Small notebook
- Poster tube or hard plastic art sleeves if you're specifically looking for posters and art

Backpacks are ideal for all-day wear, but cross-body messenger bags can be nice, too. Don't hesitate to ask an older family member to help you tote your stuff around. And please, oh please, wear comfortable shoes. You'll be doing a lot of walking and standing, so be prepared for it.

CONVENTION SPOTLIGHT

PAX UNPLUGGED

Sometimes conventions inspire the creation of spin-off conventions, as with PAX Unplugged, a show all about tabletop games. The creators of the *Penny Arcade* webcomic created the first PAX (originally called Penny Arcade Expo) in 2004 because they wanted a convention exclusively for gaming. PAX took off with tens of thousands of attendees flocking to the convention for an overload of gaming content. The tabletop gaming vertical at PAX conventions grew so popular that it inspired PAX Unplugged, held for the first time in 2017. The annual event features tournaments, live RPG events, panels about topics like why players take so long to make their next move in board games, and much more.

TIPS

What's the most exciting aspect of conventions for you?

Definitely getting to meet the fans in person. It's always nice to be able to engage with people online, but meeting them and putting faces to usernames is such a treat—especially because most of the time, people who attend conventions are just bursting with enthusiasm and joy for the properties they're into. It's really rewarding to be able to contribute to their happiness in some small way, even if it's just drawing a cover for their favorite book or designing an accessory that they can hold on to for years to come.   **—Jen Bartel**

What conventions should I attend?

If you can, talk to someone who has attended the convention before. If you don't know anyone personally, there are a lot of blog posts and podcast episodes offering advice for first-time con-goers. My biggest advice is to wear comfortable shoes, dress in layers (rooms can be very different temperatures), and remember to eat food and drink water!   **—Jordan Dené Ellis**

What tips do you have for kids going to their first-ever convention?

There will be so much that you want to do and see, but there won't be enough time in the day to do it all. For instance, a photo op with your favorite actor might be happening at the same time as a panel with the people from your favorite show. You're going to have to make some hard choices about which things you feel you absolutely cannot miss and which things you'll be comfortable waiting until the next convention for. And don't forget to have fun!   —**Liz Crowder Serota**

How do I pass the time while waiting in lines?

You'll be waiting in a queue at some point during a convention, so accept it before you arrive and bring patience with you. If you feel like striking up a conversation with those around you, go for it. If not, that's fine, too. I recommend bringing a book or comic to pass the time or maybe even a card game (one you can play alone or with others). I've seen people play video games, mobile phone games, and even knit while waiting in line to get into a panel. Just remember you'll need to be able to pick up and keep moving when the line progresses.   —**Amy Ratcliffe**

■ ■ ■ ■

As you gear up for your first convention, you might stumble across some words, phrases, or other things you don't know. That's okay! We have a glossary on page 125 to help you with all the convention basics.

The End of This Story

(and the Beginning of Your Journey in Fandom)

THROW UP YOUR HAND FOR a high five. You've just learned a ton about what makes being a fan incredible *and* how to express yourself within your fandoms. The tips and advice in this book will help you take your first steps into the larger geeky world, and now you're ready to cosplay, to start that podcast, to pen your own fanfic, and so much more. Never forget that your contributions will help make your fandoms stronger and more unique because no one else is creative in the same ways that you are.

As time goes on and you grow and explore the vast pop culture ecosystem, your contributions, like your fandom, will fluctuate and change. Maybe at some point, you'll be interested in designing RPGs instead of just playing them. Or you'll discover that you want to be a cosplay photographer rather than a cosplayer. That's all okay. Be flexible, and follow your passions wherever they take you. Your favorite fandoms might change, and new fandoms will come along and fill your heart with joy. The great news is that there will always be new characters, stories, worlds, and creators for you to discover, enjoy, and share. Sometimes you'll wonder how you can even hold so many fandoms so close to your heart.

Remember, fandom and their communities are always growing and changing. World events will affect them, conventions will come and go, and technological advances influence how you'll create and share your work. Your communities will add new members and lose some others along the way, but always cherish those friends and people who "get" you and the things you love. Stand up, be brave, and be bold to make sure that every community that you are a part of is a welcoming, thoughtful, and fun space. Remember, it's like Uncle Iroh says in *Avatar: The Last Airbender*: "It is important to draw wisdom from many different places." So when these changes happen, take them as a chance to explore and learn, and know that your fandom will always be yours no matter what.

Pave the path to ultimate fandom joy with these steps:

- Start that cosplay, that fanart, whatever it is. Even if it's scary, do it.
- Stay curious about your fandoms and communities.
- Hold your fandom to high standards. You deserve the very best.
- Be kind to new fans.
- Be comfortable.
- Be yourself.
- Be a fan.

THIS IS MY FANDOM! SHEET

So, you know you're a fan, but what does your fandom look like?
Complete this sheet and find out.

When I think about TV series, movies, games, and books I love, this one pops into my head first: _____

_____

_____

That's one of your fandoms—maybe your primary or only one!

Where does this story take place? _____

_____

_____

_____

_____

_____

_____

_____

_____

_____

The characters I can't get enough of in this story are: _____

_____

_____

_____

_____

_____

_____

_____

_____

_____

_____

_____

Why do I feel emotionally invested in this fandom? _____

_____

_____

_____

_____

_____

_____

_____

_____

_____

_____

_____

_____

In one sentence, I would describe my thoughts about this fandom as: _____

_____

_____

I want to make my own place in this fandom with (circle however many apply):
Fanart • Fanfic • Cosplay • Podcasting • Games • Community-building • Conventions

Pick one of the items you circled. Write down the first steps you'll take to make

it happen. _____

_____

_____

_____

_____

_____

_____

_____

_____

_____

_____

_____

_____

_____

FAN CHARACTER SHEET

Let's talk about your three favorite characters across all your fandoms.

My favorite characters are: _____

_____
_____
_____
_____
_____
_____
_____
_____
_____
_____
_____
_____
_____

They're from these fandoms: _____

_____
_____
_____
_____
_____
_____
_____
_____
_____
_____
_____
_____
_____

I like these traits best about them: _____

_____

_____

_____

_____

_____

_____

_____

_____

_____

_____

_____

_____

_____

_____

_____

_____

_____

_____

_____

_____

_____

_____

_____

_____

_____

_____

_____

_____

_____

Choose one of these characters, and either draw yourself as that character or write a hundred words (a drabble) about them.

FANDOM GLOSSARY

Learn new, key fandom terms and revisit some concepts from throughout the book.

ALTERNATE UNIVERSE (AU)

Alternate universes encompass stories and art that take place or feature a character outside of the established canon.

CANON

The approved, official source material for the fictional universe you adore. Canon can be closed (when all the material is completed) or open (when material isn't finished or released yet).

COMPRESSION

Applying compression to your podcasting audio file will bring the quietest sections and loudest sections of your audio closer together for more consistent volume.

CONNUI

Formed from the words "con" and "ennui," connui is the sadness and dissatisfaction you may feel when you leave a convention and come back to the real world.

COSPLAY CONTEST

Conventions often hold cosplay contests where cosplayers can sign up in certain categories, show off their ensemble at an event, and have the opportunity to win prizes.

FANDOM

Fandom is a community of people who are fans of someone or something. People started using the term in the early twentieth century.

FANDOM WAR

When groups of fans argue that their fandom is better than another group's, it's called a fandom war. However, no one's fandom has more value than someone else's.

FANNISH

Fannish means of or relating to fans and fandom. If it's a fan activity, you can use the adjective fannish to describe it.

FANON

Fanon is any piece of information fans accept even though it has no factual basis in canon. Sometimes fanon facts do end up in the canon—this is known as ascended fanon.

FLUFF

Fluff is the kind of fanfic that's intended to cause warm and fuzzy feelings.

GATEKEEPING

Gatekeeping is a disrespectful circumstance that sometimes happens in fandom. This is when a person or a group limits access to a fandom, usually based on subjective rules.

GATEWAY GAME

Whichever game first got you into gaming (video, tabletop, or role-playing), that's known as your gateway game.

HEAD CANON

When the canon leaves a question unanswered or a circumstance unexplained, fanfic can fill in head canon (sometimes called personal canon). The fanfic author's interpretation or belief about the canon is head canon.

MAINSTREAM

When something is mainstream, it is widely known and accepted not only by fans but by people outside of the fandom's community.

MASH-UP

A mash-up costume takes elements of characters' costumes from two or more fandoms to craft something completely new and creative. This can also be called a crossover.

MIXING DOWN

When you record multiple tracks while podcasting and combine those tracks into a single audio file, you're mixing down.

MOD

Short for modification, mod is when you alter an existing piece of clothing or an accessory for cosplay. It is also used in game development when you make an addition or alteration of the rules or a certain part of a current game.

OTAKU

In Japanese, otaku means "your house." But in fandom, it's a kind of synonym for "geek." An otaku is someone who is passionate about Japanese pop culture, usually anime or manga.

PEACE BOND

If your cosplay has a prop weapon, conventions will inspect it and apply a peace bond (usually a zip tie) so that you can't draw the weapon at the convention.

PLAYTEST

To playtest a game means to check for design flaws and make sure the rules make sense for the gameplay.

RETCON

The canon establishes a timeline and plot, but if you want to alter those things slightly or enrich them in your fanfic, you're retconning them.

SHIPPING

To ship is to imagine two specific characters in a romantic relationship. Derived from the word relationship, shipping in fanfic means you write two people as a pairing.

SIGNAL BOOST

When someone asks for a signal boost, they're asking you to share something through your own communities and networks. That could be in person or posting it on social media or in a forum.

TPTB

Standing for "the powers that be," this refers to creators behind any given fandom. This includes anyone who has a hand in generating a fandom's canon.

UNDERGROUND

An underground work is generally seen as more experimental and as an alternative to more well-known, popular things and is known by a small group of fans or specific audiences.

VENDOR

The merchandisers selling items at conventions are known as vendors; the areas vendors sell from are called booths.

WORBLA

A popular thermoplastic modeling material used by cosplayers.

EXTRA MATERIALS AND RESOURCES

Deputize an older family member to check these online resources and expand your fandom and communities.

FANFIC

Archive of Our Own (AO3)—https://archiveofourown.org/

Dive into hours and hours of reading fanfic. Maybe some of the stories you read will inspire you. Keep a journal on hand to take notes on whatever grabs your attention.

Fanfic Mind Map worksheet—https://howtowritefanfiction.com/worksheets/mind-map-worksheet/

Get that brainstorming on with a mind map. Use this handy worksheet to organize your thoughts.

FANART

Creative Bloq—https://www.creativebloq.com/

Satisfy your craving for art inspiration and how-tos with this site. They have practically endless information to stoke your artistic fire.

Tumblr—https://www.tumblr.com/search/fan+art

Instagram—https://www.instagram.com/explore/tags/fanart/?hl=en

There's a whole wide world of fanart out there. Look around, get ideas, and then go make your own art.

GIMP—https://www.gimp.org/

Dig into digital art with this free photo editing and manipulation software.

FANZINES

Canva—https://www.canva.com/

Use this free tool to design killer zine layouts.

WEBCOMICS

LINE Webtoon—https://www.webtoons.com/en/

Find a ton of webcomics to enjoy.

COSPLAY

Cosplay.com—https://cosplay.com/

See finished costumes, gather reference materials, and learn handy tips all in one place.

The Replica Prop Forum—https://www.therpf.com/forums/

RPF members post insanely helpful guides and in-process photos for all sorts of costumes. This is a wonderful place to learn and ask any questions you have.

Kamui Cosplay video tutorials—https://www.youtube.com/user /Mogrymillian/videos

Kamui Cosplay, a super-talented professional cosplayer, shares very straightforward tutorials through her YouTube channel. These are especially useful if you plan on making any kind of armor.

PODCASTING

Podcast Insights—https://www.podcastinsights.com/

How-to guides, equipment information, reviews, and general show guidance—this site collects it all.

Audacity—https://www.audacityteam.org/

You'll need audio software to edit your podcast, and you can download Audacity for free.

Libsyn—https://libsyn.com/

> When you're ready to share your podcast with a bigger audience, look into Libsyn for podcast hosting.

GAMING

Game Guides—https://guides.gamepressure.com/

> Stuck in a tough place in a video game? There is absolutely nothing wrong with turning to the web for help. This site has guides for about a million different games.

Dungeons & Dragons resources—https://dnd.wizards.com/products /tabletop-games/trpg-resources

> If you're dipping your toes into the D&D water, visit Wizard of the Coast's resources page to add some strength to your saving throw.

Dave's Mapper—https://davesmapper.com/

> Who doesn't love maps? Here you can take control of an easy-to-use map tool to create the perfect map to accompany your RPG adventures.

BoardGameGeek—https://boardgamegeek.com/

> Level up your board game knowledge with detailed overviews and reviews. You can also ask questions and discuss your favorite board games in this site's forums.

CONVENTIONS

Convention Scene—https://www.conventionscene.com/

> Find more conventions at Convention Scene than you can shake a cosplay sword at. But only shake the sword if it's made of foam, okay?

Acknowledgments

I am overflowing with gratitude for the opportunity to write this book. Fandom has been so important in my life, and I hope this guide helps kids and adults forge stronger connections with the stories they love. I want to give special thanks to my editor, Britny Brooks-Perilli, for working with me on this dream of a project and bringing so much insight and thoughtfulness to this book—and for recommending several new stories for me to love along the way (everyone should read Rachel Smythe's *Lore Olympus*!). I also want to thank my agent, Eric Smith of P.S. Literary Agency, for being the best cheerleader and champion an author could ask for. I am hugely grateful to Marissa Raybuck for designing this book and to Dave Perillo for bringing his striking, gorgeous illustrations to the party. My many thanks to Valerie Howlett and Isabella Nugent for helping me share this book with the world. I am so appreciative to Running Press Kids for letting me gush about fandom in this way. Finally, I am indebted to the many wonderful fictional universes that have helped shape who I am and connected me with so many other fans. Fandom is kinda the best.

— ABOUT —
THE AUTHOR

Amy Ratcliffe is part of many fandoms, including *Star Wars*, *The Witcher*, and anything Tolkien. She's cosplayed as Han Solo and Merida. She's the author of *Star Wars: Women of the Galaxy* and *Star Wars: Elee and Me*. She's the managing editor for *Nerdist*, a host, and an entertainment reporter. Based in Los Angeles with her husband and two cats, she's always looking forward to the next time she eats pizza.

— ABOUT —
THE ILLUSTRATOR

Dave Perillo is an illustrator and designer based out of the Philadelphia suburbs. With the help of an Ed Emberly drawing book, hours of cartoons, and a "healthy" diet of sugary cereals, he doodled his way through school and on to college to study graphic design. His first position was as an illustrator in the glamorous world of medical publishing. After countless drawings of dancing kidneys and otoscopes, he felt a need to feed his creative juices and began to create his own pop culture–inspired art. This path launched him into a world of comic conventions, art galleries, and freelance design. He developed his retro art style and use of a limited color palette from his love of the mid-century modern aesthetic. Dave has done work for many prestigious clients including Disney, Marvel, Target, Lucasfilm, Pixar, Nickelodeon, and Cartoon Network, to name a few. To see more of Dave's work, check out www.daveperilloart.com.